The Two W's of Journalism

The Why and What
of Public Affairs Reporting

LEA'S COMMUNICATION SERIES
Jennings Bryant/Dolf Zillmann, General Editors

Selected titles in Journalism (Maxwell McCombs, Advisory Editor) include:

Bunker • Critiquing Free Speech: First Amendment Theory and the Challenge of Interdisciplinarity

Garrison • Professional Feature Writing, Fourth Edition

Heider • White News: Why Local News Programs Don't Cover People of Color

Merrill/Gade/Blevens • Twilight of Press Freedom: The Rise of People's Journalism

Merritt • Public Journalism and Public Life: Why Telling the News is Not Enough, Second Edition

Wanta • The Public and the National Agenda: How People Learn About Important Issues

---

For a complete list of titles in LEA's Communication Series, please contact Lawrence Erlbaum Associates, Publishers at www.erlbaum.com

The Two W's of Journalism

The Why and What
of Public Affairs Reporting

Davis Merritt
Author
"Public Journalism and Public Life:
Why Telling the News is Not Enough"

Maxwell McCombs
University of Texas at Austin

LAWRENCE ERLBAUM ASSOCIATES, PUBLISHERS

2004   Mahwah, New Jersey   London

Lawrence Erlbaum Associates, Inc., Publishers
10 Industrial Avenue
Mahwah, NJ 07430

Cover design by Sean Sciarrone

Library of Congress Cataloging-in-Publication Data

Merritt Davis.
The two W;s of journalism : the why and what of public affairs journalism /
    Davis "Buzz" Merritt and Maxwell McCombs.
        p.   cm.   (LEA's communication series)
    Includes bibliographical references and index.
ISBN 0-8058-4730-8 (cloth : alk. paper)
ISBN 0-8058-4731-6 (pbk. : alk. paper)
1. Journalism—Political aspects—United States.   2. Journalism—Social
    aspects—United States.   I. McCombs, Maxwell E.   II. Title.   III. Series.
PN4888 2003.P6M39 2004
071'.3—dc21   2003046233
                                                                      CIP

Books published by Lawrence Erlbaum Associates are printed on acid-free paper, and their bindings are chosen for strength and durability.

Printed in the United States of America
10 9 8 7 6 5 4 3 2 1

To Libby, for all the reasons she knows
—Davis Merritt

For Betsy and my children, Molly,
Leslie, Max, and Sam
—Max McCombs

Contents

About the Authors

Davis "Buzz" Merritt was a reporter and editor for Knight Newspapers and Knight Ridder Inc. for 43 years, retiring after 23 years as editor of The Wichita Eagle. Since leaving The Eagle, he has taught media ethics and a seminar on journalism and democracy at the University of Kansas and Wichita State University, consulted with news organizations and written articles, newspaper columns, and books. He wrote the seminal book on public journalism, Public Journalism and Public Life: Why Telling the News Is Not Enough, published by Lawrence Erlbaum Associates. The 1996 second edition received a citation from Pennsylvania State University for media criticism.

Maxwell McCombs, who is internationally recognized for his research on the agenda-setting role of mass communication, holds the Jesse H. Jones Centennial Chair in Communication at the University of Texas at Austin and is a professor on the associated faculty of Catholic University in Santiago, Chile. Prior to joining the Texas faculty, McCombs was the John Ben Snow Professor of Research at Syracuse University and also served simultaneously for 10 years as director of the News Research Center of the American Newspaper Publishers Association. McCombs has been on the faculties of the University of North Carolina and U.C.L.A. and a reporter for the New Orleans Times-Picayune.

Preface

Public affairs journalism is a subcategory of all journalism, but it lies at the core of the profession because the practice of journalism is, finally, inseparable from the practice of democracy. Doing journalism of any sort requires two important sets of talents—reporting the news and presenting the news. For the most part, journalists' understanding of how to report the most relevant events and situations of the moment is based on the traditions and routines expressed in news values and news beats. Those notions of how to present this news also are grounded in the honed norms and routines of the newsroom.

Implementing these two sets of talents largely defines the working days of professional journalists. Teaching these talents to future journalists largely defines the working days of professors in journalism schools. In neither situation is there much time left over to reflect on why journalism does its work in these particular ways even though the current modes of reporting and presenting the news are far from the only available options.

Increasingly, questions are asked about whether these talents are being put to the best possible use. In some cases, these questions even suggest that the current implementation of these talents has significant negative consequences for society.

The purpose of this book is considerably more than to add another voice to the critical chorus. Rather, its purpose is to probe the foundations of public affairs journalism, to bring to the forefront the core professional question of "why do we do it?" and then to build on the goals identified there by asking "what are the ways of fulfilling those goals?"

For newsrooms, the aim of this book is to stimulate the examination of contemporary practice in light of these foundations. In the classroom, the aim of this book is to complement reporting, editing and news writing textbooks and the essential training in journalistic skills with a detailed understanding of journalism's larger end. As the nation settles into this new century and its cacophony of journalistic voices, explicit elaboration of the foundations of journalism is essential in both of these settings.

Introduction

As a new century began on January 1, 2000, technology presented journalists—and potentially every other person—almost instantaneous access to a crush of information, data, facts and events that, as Neil Postman wrote, create "a world of fragments and discontinuities; a neighborhood of strangers and pointless quantity."[1]

Journalists assume the formidable task of telling other people which tiny portion of those events, facts and data matter the most and how they matter. From constant informational chaos, a thing journalists call "news" is sorted out by the process of journalistic choice, a set of decisions about what matters and why, which are based in the judgment and values of the journalists making those decisions.

That is a daunting enough task in itself, but this age of Internet access and nonjournalists' expanding skills at seeking information on their own complicates the challenge for journalists. Traditional journalistic vehicles—newspapers, magazines and broadcasting—no longer have a monopoly as mediators, filters, organizers and interpreters.

So one of the central questions for 21st century society in general and journalists in particular is this: What mediating devices, what filters, and, most important, which values will become the prevailing ones in sorting relevance out of that overwhelming flood of information? The question is crucial because to govern itself and deal with its problems, a democratic society needs a body of shared, relevant information and an effective forum for discussing the implications of that information. Otherwise, the conversation and deliberation that are essential to a functioning free society cannot exist.

Where will the body of shared information and the forum for discussing it be found in the new millennium? If journalists do not provide it, who will?

WHAT WAS ...

Well before the explosion of the Information age, a perceived need for consistency in judgment led traditional journalists to adopt a set of filters that are, in

---

[1]Neil Postman, *Amusing ourselves to death*. New York: Penguin Books, 1985, p. 70.

fact, values. They came to be accepted as news values, that is, the criteria by which the relative importance of events is sorted out. The usual list includes timeliness, conflict, impact or relevance, novelty, prominence of the people or institutions involved, and proximity of the audience to the event.

The list is a pragmatic one, consisting of elements that, alone or in combination, constitute what will be reported as news. The list is delimiting; that is, not every bit of information that is available or every event that occurs falls within its scope. For instance, a newly discovered fact about a historic event will not be rendered as news unless it also meets one or more of the other standards; and something out of the ordinary that happens to you or me may not be news but when the same thing happens to a prominent person may be passed along as such.

But the list, while traditional and widely accepted, hardly exhausts all the possibilities. Television, for instance, insists on another element: visuality. Although visuality has no connection with relevance or timeliness or the other traditional criteria, it is clearly a value filter that television news directors routinely use in deciding what to broadcast. Likewise, breadth of movement and degree of interconnectivity are critical to Web site design and become other value filters that affect and structure content.

It is an unavoidable fact that the values we as journalists apply to the flow of available information—what we choose to pass along—set the agenda for the public conversation that drives and nurtures democracy. This book about reporting and editing suggests adding an overriding value to the traditional list of news values that are used to filter relevance from irrelevance.

The overriding value is that for democracy to succeed and prosper (and not incidentally, continue to tolerate and nurture journalistic freedom), people must be broadly and deeply engaged in it. And to be engaged, people need shared, relevant information. That is, they need agreed-on facts on which to base a conversation aimed at answering the fundamental question of democracy: "What shall we do?" Without a body of shared, relevant facts, that conversation cannot have coherence and accomplish its goal.

WHAT IS ...

While technology makes more and more of the endless chaos of events accessible, technology itself is nonjudgmental about relative importance. Data, facts and information do not frame themselves or explain their meaning. And the more data, facts and information that come to hand, the more important and difficult becomes the task of framing them into shared relevance and applicability.

The information explosion, which began with Samuel F. B. Morse's patient language of dots and dashes, and in slightly more than a century grew to the point of instantaneous access to virtually any known fact, turned information into a commodity. As Postman noted in "Amusing Ourselves To Death," this commodity became "a 'thing' that could be bought and sold irrespective of its uses or meanings."[2] Henry David Thoreau reflected an understanding of this conversion of information into a "'thing' that could be bought or sold irrespective of its ... meanings" when he wrote in "Walden" in 1854:

> We are in a great haste to construct a magnetic telegraph from Maine to Texas; but Maine and Texas, it may be, have nothing important to communicate. ... We are eager to tunnel under the Atlantic and bring the old world some weeks nearer to the new; but perchance the first news that will leak through into the broad flapping American ear will be that Princess Adelaide has the whooping cough."[3]

Both Postman and Thoreau were suggesting that the new commodity would be a mixed blessing, its ultimate value wholly dependent on how people managed it. Both were concerned that the information monster would impose on humanity its own artificial version of community and conversation and sensibility; that information would be confused with knowledge and knowledge with wisdom. They were right to be concerned, for it's happening, and the greatest challenge to journalists in this new century will be to make sure that the information monster serves people rather than defines them, that we do not lose in the flood of bits and bytes the values that bind us as communities of interest, and that we have the skill and will to identify and frame the shared relevance that will allow citizens to carry on the deliberations that are essential to a successful democracy.

Recognizing that challenge, David Shenk wrote, "New information for its own sake is no longer a goal worthy of our best reporters, our best analysts, our best minds. Journalists will need to take a more holistic approach to information as a natural resource that has to be managed more than acquired."[4] Holism accepts that the whole is more than the sum of its individual parts. The foundation of this book's approach to reporting and editing is that the responsibility of the journalist in the age of information glut extends beyond the mere accumulation and organization of information. The responsibility is larger than the sum of its parts, and includes presenting information in ways that help citizens and communities see common interests and the possibilities of common approaches to problem-solving. These are the essence of democracy.

This approach to reporting and editing does not abandon the most valued aspects of traditional news gathering such as fairness, accuracy, what is known as journalistic objectivity, timeliness and importance. It applies

---

[2]Postman, *Amusing ourselves to death*, p. 65.

[3]Quoted in Postman, *Amusing ourselves to death*, p. 65.

[4]David Shenk, *Data smog: Surviving the information glut.* New York: Harper Collins, 1997, p. 170.

those values—and adds some new ones—in a broader context. It is designed to equip journalists not only with a set of techniques (the what) but also with a public purpose (the why). In that sense, it recaptures some of the character and flavor of American journalism's early history that has been wrung out of the profession over recent decades by many forces.

Journalism, in any technological iteration, and democracy are fully interdependent. Neither can exist without the other. If journalism and democracy are to prosper together, journalists must fully understand that they are stakeholders in both, must see the interdependence of the two and make their filtering decisions with that interdependence always in mind.

The genius of democracy is that, over time and with much tugging and hauling, things get done and issues get resolved. The central question "What shall we do?"—is answered. The concept of self-determination and individual freedom wrapped into the idea of public will and majority rule makes a powerful combination that has kept democracy alive in the United States despite many bumps and detours along the way.

Those bumps and detours are inevitable because the political expression of democracy is carried out by individuals who bring to the activity vastly different, often competing—and sometimes unhealthy—values and motivations. The push-and-pull of politics can be messy, discouraging, cynicism-inspiring and, at times, simply ugly. Contemporary journalism's daily and weekly focus on that part of the process to the exclusion of the broader picture leads both journalists and citizens into the mistaken and shortsighted conclusion that the process is impenetrable and will inevitably be the captive of special interests. Analysis restricted to the short term certainly bears out that sad conclusion with great frequency, but a political process that did not allow such freewheeling competition of ideas and interests would not be truly free.

The messiness is an unavoidable part of the process, but we must keep constantly in mind that this is not the whole process. The clear and present danger to democracy is not that it is messy, or that charlatans can be involved in it, or that corruption and intellectual dishonesty often seem to dominate. The clear and present danger is that we—as journalists and citizens—give up on it and leave the field to those interlopers.

There is a viable alternative to surrender, and that is what this book is about. Tools and philosophies exist to frame a practice of journalism that keeps its focus on the vital larger picture and helps citizens maintain and strengthen their hold on what is rightly theirs in a democracy.

WHAT CAN BE ...

Public affairs journalism in the information-rich 21st century will require at every level of its practice broader skills as well as a broader philosophy. The skills requirement arises because of the swift and certain convergence of varying forms of news presentation and the pressures presented by the possibility of instant, worldwide communication of that news. The creations of reporters, editors and other presentation specialists can no longer be targeted at one medium—newspapers, for instance. Journalists will be expected to provide content for print, online and broadcasting at the same time.

The requirement for a broader philosophy than "it happened, so it's news" arises out of the very technological explosion that allows us to know about a myriad of things and events every moment. The more things we are aware of, the more complex the task of deciding what facts to pass along and how to frame them. In particular, this has huge implications for the news media's unquestioned agenda-setting function in society, a topic that is discussed in Chapter 5 (this volume).

Jay Rosen of New York University summed up the need for a more purposeful journalistic philosophy this way: "History has sometimes been called the search for a usable past. Journalism at its best can be a search for a usable present."[5]

Usable means at least two things in this formulation: that individuals will find it useful and that what is reported about public affairs will keep public life viable and engaging. The authors believe that journalism in recent years has not been usable within those meanings; that journalism is, uniquely among American institutions, free to define itself; and that a substantial re-definition is needed for journalism to become truly usable. This book is about the search for that re-definition of usable, significant news.

---

[5]Jay Rosen, *The master of its own domain*, www.Intellectualcapital.com (5-11-00)

Part I

CHAPTER
1

The Why

Public life is the way democracy is expressed and experienced. Most people, willingly or unwillingly, must interact with others to accomplish their personal goals, assert their individual rights and promote their private interests as well as the collective public interest.

Shared information is the key to that transaction, and how people behave in that interaction depends on how they apply their core values to the information that they acquire. Because core values vary over a wide spectrum and because information is acquired unevenly and from many sources, the process of public life is unavoidably raucous and stressful. Two individuals frequently approach the same issue with totally different value sets and totally different information. Given the high likelihood of differing value and information contexts when two or more people come together, why does public life nevertheless proceed at a more or less steady pace and not fall apart? The answer lies in the fact that in a democracy, most people share one fundamental value: a belief in democracy itself.

Beyond that starting point, however, lies only honest dispute. The basic question that democracy seeks to answer is "What shall we do?" about a given situation. The possible answers to that question are as complex and varied as the range of private values held and information acquired.

Two friends have agreed to take in a movie on Thursday night, but they know on Thursday afternoon that they have a problem. John favors action films and uses them as an escape from the rigors of his professional life. Mary prefers docudramas that broaden her knowledge of history and challenge her intellect, and she is put off by violence. They want to be together that evening, however, so they must resolve the clash of values to accomplish their shared goal without undue discomfort for either.

They need two things: information and, because they work in different offices, a place or way to discuss the matter.

Each has read reviews of the movies that they and the other favor and has looked at the newspaper advertisements for them: "*Amadeus*," about the life and music of Mozart and "*Ninja*," about breaking up a drug cartel in Hong Kong. Other movie choices also exist. They know the cost and the times of the movies, so they have the information they need. They will meet over coffee at 3 p.m. to decide, so they have a method for discussing the matter.

They have choices to make, and each choice has consequences. Each can insist on his or her movie preference and not spend the evening together, which neither wants. One can simply give in to the other and thus spend a less-than-enjoyable evening. One can persuade the other about his or her preference and risk offense if the argument is based on poor information or is not honestly made. They can agree on a compromise choice of movies.

They can decide to do something else altogether.

This careful weighing of choices and consequences, consideration of others' concerns and thinking about possible alternatives is called *deliberation*, and it is at the heart of democratic decision making. If John and Mary successfully resolve their disagreement, they also will accomplish something else. They will strengthen their relationship by creating what in the abstract is termed *joint social capital* and bank an experience of which they can draw in the future when the decision might be far more crucial than what movie to see. If, on the other hand, both stubbornly insist on the original choices, their relationship will be damaged and perhaps destroyed.

The way in which a potential decision is talked about sometimes becomes just as important as the decision itself because the people involved have an interest in continuing the relationship that is considerably more important than merely prevailing on a single issue. Choices on important public matters contain the same risk-and-reward factors. A community or state or nation that makes its choices through a deliberative process likewise builds civic capital, a reserve of democratic good will and success that enriches both individuals and the total society.

In one form or another and at increasing levels of complexity and consequence, that's how democracy at its best works. With the tragic exception of the Civil War, democracy in the United States has worked that way for two and a quarter centuries. The constitutional framework has not substantially changed, and even those changes, which are embodied in 27 amendments, were made through the constitutional process itself.

This long-running, continuing experiment hardly has been straight-line or smooth, nor could it have been. In a nation whose foundation stones are pulled together from every corner of the world and every political and religious belief, the only certainty is that there will be constant clashes of values and consistently different ideas about how to answer the question, "What

shall we do?" But the mortar that has held those many and varied stones together has been made up of three essential elements: shared, relevant information; a method or place for discussing the implications of that
information; and shared values on which to base a decision.

SHARED RELEVANCE

As the nation has grown from a group of sparsely populated, agrarian colonies strung along the East Coast to today's highly technological nation of
300 million, access to relevant information has become at once more efficient and less effective. Technological change, from the first telegraph message to today's astonishing cable and Internet activity, makes an endless
amount of information instantly and continuously available. This has turned
out to be a very mixed blessing.

Postman's analysis of information overload describes the problem as one
of growing impotence:

> In both oral and typographical cultures, information derives its importance from the
> possibilities of action.... But the situation created by telegraphy, and then exacerbated
> by later technologies, made the relationship between information and action both ab-
> stract and remote. For the first time in human history, people were faced with the prob-
> lem of information glut, which means that simultaneously they were faced with the
> problem of diminished social and political potency.... For the first time we were sent
> information which answered no question we had asked, and which, in any case, did
> not permit the right of reply.... Thus to the reverent question posed by Morse—what
> hath God wrought?—a disturbing answer came back: a neighborhood of strangers
> and pointless quantity; a world of fragments and discontinuities.[1]

For most of the nation's history, journalists provided much of the information to fuel democratic deliberation, first in newspapers, then also in
broadcast. Americans relied on them to sort out relevance from irrelevance,
and as journalists made those many decisions about content, they were, pur-
posefully or not, helping set the agenda for public discussion. Even into the
1950s, the origins of shared information were relatively few: a dozen major
newspapers, two wire services, three broadcast networks and a handful of
news magazines. As late as 1963, the state of information technology was
such that one can see, in grainy kinescopes of the coverage of President John
F. Kennedy's assassination, a network announcer holding a telephone up
against a desk microphone in an effort to get the words of a reporter in Dallas instantly out to the nation.

Only 30 years later, Americans were able to be anywhere at any time,
live. They watched live television from Iraq as U.S. rockets rained down on

---

[1]Postman, *Amusing ourselves to death*, pp. 68–70.

Baghdad, and they logged onto their computers to witness the birth of a baby provided in real time on a personal Web site by the proud parents. And the Internet provided a second major change. Any person with access to a computer modem—more than half of all Americans—is no longer merely a recipient of information but is also a potential information provider at many different levels, exponentially increasing the number of places from which people can receive information.

When any person on earth can theoretically reach every other person on earth with any message whatsoever—be it benign or arousing, accurate or wildly inaccurate, libelous or innocuous, profane or spiritual—the problem of providing relevance for the democratic deliberative process becomes profound.

Evidence that Postman's "world of fragments and discontinuities" had indeed arrived and that it has large consequences for the democratic process was clearly seen in the summer of 1998 as the United States struggled with the misadventures of President Bill Clinton. The conventional reporter–source dynamic was at work full blast as journalists attempted to cover the widespread official investigations of the president. They covered the daily briefings and announcements, of course, and developed leaks from official sources on both sides. All this provided a crush of information. But a new set of players inserted themselves into the game. Private Web sites posted all sorts of material, some of it wildly speculative and even wholly falsified, which had the patina of legitimacy because it was "published." Newspapers and broadcast networks with their own Web sites on occasion used different, and lower, standards of verification in deciding what to "publish" on those sites.

The informational clutter left the conscientious citizen totally bewildered and struggling to sort relevance from irrelevance. For many, the most comfortable response was withdrawal. Postman's "relationship between information and action" had indeed become abstract and remote, and in public opinion surveys a majority of Americans said they didn't want any more information about Clinton's affair; they simply wanted the matter settled.

It is easy to understand from those months in the summer of 1998 both the problem of information glut and the challenge it presents for journalists, not only in dealing with its volume, but also in gaining the attention of people who are under constant bombardment from all sides. In *"Data Smog,"* Shenk offered this admonition:

> Such a world necessitates a restructured value system in which sharing and summarizing existing information is more of a priority than is stumbling onto genuinely new data. New information for its own sake is no longer a goal worthy of our best reporters, our best analysts, our best minds. Journalists will need to take a more holistic approach to information as a natural resource that has to be *managed* more than *acquired.*

What we need now is not so much *news* but shared understanding. Who has relevant information and who needs it? We must learn to share information with one another, to manage it thoughtfully, and to transform it into universal knowledge.[2]

For journalists to provide shared relevance for the process of democratic decision making in a world full of potential irrelevance will require a different answer to the question, "What are journalists for?" It will involve, as Shenk suggested, a "restructured value system" in which journalists understand that the *why* of providing that relevance is just as important as the *how* and the *what*.

THE METHOD

As noted earlier, the second requirement for democracy to function is a method or place for citizens to discuss the information they have acquired. Technology has also vastly expanded—and complicated—that task. Whether on talk radio or television, in Internet chat rooms, in town meetings (electronic and otherwise), through e-mail or personal Web-sites, the opportunities for exchange of views have multiplied at a breathtaking pace. The dilemma is that increased opportunities for separate conversations do not automatically mean more people are involved in "*common*" conversations. This fragmentation makes social consensus difficult to recognize.

If merely providing new information is no longer a sufficient role for journalists to play in public life, what is a more useful role? In his introduction to "*The Power of News*," Michael Schudson issued this invitation:

Imagine a world ... where governments, businesses, lobbyists, candidates, churches, and social movements deliver information directly to citizens on home computers. Journalism is momentarily abolished. Citizens tap into any information source they want on the computer networks.... The Audubon Society, the Ku Klux Klan, criminals in prison, children at summer camp, elderly people in rest homes, the urban homeless and the rural recluse send and receive messages. Each of us is our own journalist. What would happen? ... People would want ways to sort through the endless information available. What is most important? What is most relevant? What is most interesting? People would want help interpreting and explaining events.... A demand would rise not only for indexers and abstracters but for interpreters, reporters, editors.... Journalism—of some sort—would be reinvented.[3]

We are not so far from that theoretical world as we might think, and the large question that looms is, "What sort of journalism will work in such an environment?"

---

[2]Shenk, "*Data smog*," p. 170.

[3]Michael Schudson, "*The power of news*." Cambridge, MA: Harvard University Press, 1995, p. 1.

Part II of this book strives to answer that question, to suggest ideas for breaking through the crush of information and multiple levels of conversation to create the shared relevance on which people can base their answers to the core question of democracy, "What shall we do?" Those ideas grow out of the belief elaborated in this portion of the book that journalists in the 21st century will need to be as adept at supporting useful deliberation and as skilled in building civic capital as they are at gathering and interpreting facts.

THE VALUES

As readers shall see, extensive research shows that people base their opinions much more on values than on factual information. The process of reaching public judgment on an issue necessarily involves bouncing facts and ideas against values and beliefs. In a country with people representing a huge variety of ethnic, religious and educational backgrounds, how can journalism possibly deal with the array of personal, often subtle values that people bring to their consideration of issues?

The answer is twofold: It cannot and it should not. But if democracy is going to be effective, one core value must permeate journalists' thinking and guide their decisions: that democracy works best when people are broadly engaged in it. So helping people engage in democracy—through information, improved civic skills and discovered opportunities—becomes the goal and the overriding criterion for evaluating what journalists do. To accomplish that goal, we need to define journalism in some different ways.

Suggestions for Additional Reading

Neil Postman, "*Amusing ourselves to death.*" New York: Penguin Books, 1985.
Michael Schudson, "*The power of news.*" Cambridge, MA: Harvard University Press, 1995.

CHAPTER

2

First Things First: Why We Have A First Amendment

James Madison would faint dead away. Thomas Jefferson would rail once more against "putrid" content in the press. George Washington would reinsert into his farewell address the bitter condemnation of newspapers that he edited out at the last minute.

After all, it is their First Amendment to the Constitution that allows *Penthouse* magazine to print pictures of people engaged in sex, lets hate groups call for the elimination of specific races of people and frees personal Internet Web sites to instruct surfers in such things as the overthrow of the government and making and stockpiling pipe bombs. Those Founding Fathers would surely be horrified.

That those 45 words, which it can be reasonably argued were crafted as an act of federalism rather than of libertarianism, arrived at their current interpretations is a demonstration of how a vigorous democracy proceeds. During the 200-plus years since the First Amendment was adopted, the courts, governments at all levels and private citizens singly and in interest groups and associations have debated with one another and fought with their consciences and, occasionally, more physical weapons to decide how those 45 words should be understood.

So as we begin this examination of the role in a democracy of the press, that is, journalism is all its forms, it's helpful to explore why those words were first penned, what they were intended to create (a matter of continuing debate) and, most important, what rights and responsibilities they imply in an environment vastly different from the one in which they were conceived. Of particular interest for our purposes are those sparse four words, "and of the press."

GETTING FROM THERE TO HERE

The arrival of the printing press in England in 1476 is as good a place as any to begin, for that event created a problem for the monarchy and the church, the two institutions that, usually together at that time, determined the fates of society and its citizens. The relatively minor, if annoying, business of dealing with dissent was immediately magnified with the introduction of the printing press, for *heresy* and *treason* could now have a life beyond their first utterances, circulating more widely and being reproduced endlessly.

The Crown's response was to license and thereby seek to control both printing presses and books. In 1538, the Star Chamber made a crime the printing of any book without prior approval of the Crown's representatives and in 1556 began to search out and destroy unlicensed books and presses. Queen Elizabeth, in 1585, decreed that the only presses that could operate would be in Oxford, Cambridge and London and nothing could be printed without approval of the Archbishop of Canterbury and the Bishop of London. It didn't work, of course. Some brave but unfortunate writers and printers were imprisoned, had various body parts cut off (ears and hands were favorite punishments), or were executed. But the genie was out of the bottle forever, and the next century and a half saw a constant struggle over "truth"—the Crown-church version and the many versions offered by adventuresome and determined thinkers and writers.

Licensing of the press ended in England in 1695. The Enlightenment explosion of scientific discovery and philosophical fomentation as much as anything dictated that knowledge and ideas needed to be widely circulated. In 1694, John Locke, one of the Enlightenment's core figures, drafted a key document approved the next year by the House of Commons. This document argued that licensing controls were impairing the trade of printing and thus the circulation of ideas and at any rate were impractical and inconsistent in application.

The end of licensing did not, of course, mean the end of efforts to suppress ideas. The expression of heresies and treasons such as "imagining the death of the king" were still swiftly and often cruelly punished after the fact of publication. It took yet another strand of Enlightenment thinking to bring the next steps toward true freedom of expression. In 1644, John Milton's *"Areopagitica: A Speech of Mr. John Milton For the Liberty of Unlicenc'd Printing"* was published, without a license of course. In it he eloquently summed up one of the core ideas of Enlightenment thinking: that truth, given a fair chance, will always prevail over falsity. Truth does not need protection from competition of other ideas, he argued. "Let her and Falsehood grapple; who ever knew Truth put to the worse, in a free and open encounter," was his now immortal iteration of the idea that was to become the rationale for free expression.

By the 18th century, the belief that the clash of competing ideas produces better outcomes was already embedded in various ways, such as trial by jury, legislative debates and in scholarly pursuits such as scientific research. But direct offenses against the established church and state were still punishable, and the final step over the threshold of free expression would be taken only near the end of the century and across the Atlantic in the U.S. colonies.

"A REPUBLIC, IF YOU CAN KEEP IT ..."

Benjamin Franklin's oft-quoted response to the question of what sort of government had been devised by the constitutional convention in 1787 was immediately relevant. Because the convention proceedings were held in closest secrecy (even James Madison, in a letter to his close friend Thomas Jefferson, who was in Paris, refused to relay the details), the young nation was anxious to read the Constitution that the convention had produced. Negative reaction was immediate in many quarters. Delegates to the ratifying conventions in several states were alarmed at the potential strength invested in the new central government, an accretion of power they had come to loathe during the struggle to separate from England. The Constitution, they argued, established a form of government that could perhaps couple well with the various state governments: That is, the federal system it established could work. But where were the protections against an overreach of power by that central government, and particularly important from the perspective of Enlightenment philosophy, where were the specific expressions of the rights of individuals?

In a swift compromise, the Federalists, spurred on by Madison, introduced in the First Congress in 1789 a series of more than twenty amendments, twelve of which were finally approved and sent to the states for ratification. The first two as passed by Congress did not survive the ratification process, but the third and those that followed were approved and constitute our Bill of Rights. Thus, what is known now as the First Amendment achieved its primacy not from its own virtue but from the fact that not enough states approved of the original first two, which had to do with structural matters such as numbers of representatives from each state and the salaries of members of Congress.

That history, however, does not detract from the impact of today's First Amendment, which reads, "Congress shall make no law respecting an establishment of religion, or prohibiting the free exercise thereof, or abridging the freedom of speech, or of the press; or the right of the people peaceably to assemble, and to petition the Government for a redress of grievances." Other amendments protected against unreasonable search and seizure, excessive bail, self-incrimination, double jeopardy and guaranteed swift and public trial by jury, the right to bear arms and access to due process of law.

The final two adopted amendments, the Ninth and 10th, reflected Americans' generalized discomfort with the idea of investing their natural rights in any institution. The Ninth Amendment states that the enumeration of rights in the Constitution "shall not be construed to deny or disparage others retained by the people." That is, don't assume a right does not exist and does not reside in the people just because it isn't specifically mentioned. This was a bow to the idea that all rights reside in the people and no government can assume power not specifically granted to it by the people. The 10th Amendment states that powers not delegated to the United States by the Constitution nor specifically prohibited by it to the states are reserved to the states or to the people. That is, the federal government's reach was limited and specific, whereas the states' rights and the rights of the people were not, except as specified in the Constitution. The "reserve clause" was to assuage the concern that the federal government being established would become the 1,000-pound gorilla.

The fundamental concerns reflected in the Ninth and 10th Amendments have echoed through the 200 years since the Bill of Rights was finally adopted in 1791. As liberals and conservatives, Democrats and Republicans, strict constructionists and judicial activists looked to the Constitution and Bill of Rights to justify their actions and beliefs, there was plenty of ammunition for all sides.

That the dire possibility suggested by Franklin has been avoided given all the ambiguity and overlap in the document is a testament to the flexibility of the Founders' work. As one pair of commentators put it, the Founders,'

> "greatest gift to the nation may not have been the document at all, but rather the spirit of pragmatic compromise which set the precedent and tone for most future conflicts. In seeking practical solutions to relatively short-term conflicts, they were forced to be flexible. Their structure...was loose enough so that it could bend and conform to changing social institutions and political tempers."[1]

BUT WHAT DID THEY *REALLY* MEAN?

Was the First Amendment "more an act of federalism than of libertarianism," as Michael Schudson[2] argued, "and distinctly an afterthought"? Or

---

[1]David J. Olson & Philip Meyer, *"To keep the republic."* New York: McGraw-Hill, 1975, p. 37.

[2]Michael Schudson, *"The good citizen; A history of American civic life."* New York: Free Press, 1998, p. 73.

was it, as James Carey[3] suggested, "a compact description of a desirable political society," and an "attempt to define the nature of public life as it existed at the time or as the Founders hoped it would exist"?

One can have the historical intent of it either way because as a practical matter, it is what it is today, not what it was in 1791. Yet understanding how it got to where it is today and why there is still disagreement over intent is worth some effort because such is the nature of a living democracy that what exists today might well not be what exists in the years ahead.

Arguments about the meaning and import of the First Amendment's press clause were immediate and vigorous and often based in the competing views of federalism and anti-federalism as the Bill of Rights was debated. Alexander Hamilton, for instance, was hardly an opponent of a free press, but he was a government minimalist. "Why," he argued in the *Federalist* papers, "declare that things will not be done which there is no power to do?"[4] In other words, the federal government, in Hamilton's view, had no implied powers, only those implicit in the Constitution's language. Because it therefore lacked the power to control the press, why suggest that the authority might exist by referring to it? "Why for instance should it be said that the liberty of the press shall not be restrained, when no power is given by which restrictions may be imposed?"[5]

On the other hand, Richard Henry Lee argued that it was better to be safe than sorry. "All parties apparently agree that the freedom of the press is a fundamental right.... Why should not the people, in adopting a federal constitution, declare this, even if there are only doubts about it?"[6] Nine of the original ratifying states already had guarantees of press freedom in their constitutions and, it was argued by those concerned with state power over federal power, the others could do so if they chose. Madison finally carried the day, supported by the primary concern expressed by Lee that if certain civil liberties were not specifically expressed, ways to deny them might be found in the body of the Constitution itself.

So the specific admonition, "Congress shall make no law" abridging freedom of the press was set in concrete, a seemingly bright, clear line. But it took only 7 years for that line to become obscured. In 1798, the Federalist-dominated Congress narrowly passed the Sedition Act, restoring prosecutions for criminal libel, as a way to quell newspaper opposition to an anticipated war with France. The act leapt backward over the First Amendment to the British notion that although prior restraint (i.e., licensing) might be abhorrent and il-

---

[3]James Carey, "*A critical reader.*" Minneapolis: University of Minnesota Press, 1997, p. 238.

[4]Quoted in Jeffery A. Smith, "*Printers and press freedom: The ideology of early American journalism.*" New York: Oxford University Press, 1988, p. 166.

[5]Quoted in Smith, "*Printers and press freedom,*" p. 166.

[6]Quoted in Smith, "*Printers and press freedom,*" p. 166.

legal, journalists must nevertheless be prepared to pay a price should they print "anything false, scandalous or malicious" against anyone in government "with the intent to … bring them … into contempt or disrepute; or to excite against them … the hatred of the good people of the United States."

The rationale for the Sedition Act, even in the face of the First Amendment, was that the objective of a free press was to allow citizens to determine what sort of government they would live under. Once that government was established, however, words designed to undermine citizens' good opinion of that government were considered dangerous and criminal, a notion that survived well into the 20th century. In the heated political atmosphere of 1799, James Bayard declared in Congress,

> "How is that good opinion to be preserved if wicked and unprincipled men, men of inordinate and desperate ambition, are allowed to state facts to the people which are not true, which they know at the time to be false, and which are stated with the criminal intention of bringing the Government into disrepute among the people? This was falsely and deceitfully stealing the public opinion; it was a felony of the worst and most dangerous nature."[7]

Despite the protests of Madison, Jefferson and others, there were 25 prosecutions and 10 convictions by the Federalist-dominated judiciary. (Judicial review of acts of Congress had not yet been established.) This had no small impact because there were only about 200 newspapers in the nation. The act expired after the Federalists lost the presidency to Jefferson in 1800, but the misadventure reinforced public support of the First Amendment and since that time only occasional and futile efforts have been made to reintroduce the notion of seditious libel.

So the nation entered the 19th century with a press convinced of its constitutional protections and, buoyed by Milton's and Locke's soaring words about truth and its combat with falsehood, ready for that battle. Whereas the colonial press had been, for various reasons, largely neutral, the struggle for independence and then over the content and meaning of the Constitution had greatly increased both the number of newspapers and their partisanship.

We need not concern ourselves here with the details of the legal and political processes that brought our understanding of the First Amendment from the Sedition Act to its present state. They are well documented in numerous texts and analyses: a series of steps forward, backward and, sometimes, sideways, punctuated by a few particularly significant court cases. As with the interpretation of any law or constitutional paragraph, the composition of the courts and the political and social environment of the times that gave rise to the specific cases affected each of those decisions. Rather, our primary concern is broader: not merely what court interpretations of the First Amendment allow journalists to do or not do (which is forever arguable and subject to reinterpretation), but what

---

[7]Quoted in Schudson, *"The good citizen,"* pp. 73–74.

broader duties and responsibilities beyond the merely legal journalists have toward democracy that the First Amendment helps to define.

BUT WHICH "DEFINITION?"

Two contemporary commentators, Schudson in his 1998 book *"The Good Citizen,"* and Carey, in a 1995 essay *The Press, Public Opinion, and Public Discourse,* provide a useful framework of competing ideas.

Schudson[8] argued that the First Amendment and the establishment of a "free press" were "distinctly an afterthought for the leading framers of the Constitution," rather than, as it is widely believed today, intended by them to be "keystones of our entire political system and central, necessary guarantors of a democratic way of life." Schudson cited six arguments to support this view:

- The amendment limited the Congress but not the states and thus was "an act of federalism more than of libertarianism."
- Its framers distinguished between the use of the press and its abuse and that it was no longer free if it were "perverted to the uses of power."
- Passage and use of the Sedition Act demonstrates adherence to those limits.
- They were unable to even conceive of the press playing a positive, regular role in communication because of its sparse existence and combative nature at the time.
- They were regularly and severely critical of what they saw as abuses by editors.
- The *Federalist* papers, 85 in all, contain only four mentions of the press, all in passing.

Schudson conceded that in the wake of the Sedition Act, Americans "did boldly embrace a free press as a necessary bulwark of a liberal civil order," and that role took its place in "a multi-faceted drama of democratization" of the new nation. But for Schudson, the First Amendment was only one scene in that broader drama.

Carey,[9] in contrast, saw a more organic origin and purpose in the founder's words:

> Today, we generally read the First Amendment as a loose collection of clauses: religion, assembly, speech, and press. Read against the background of public life, however, the First Amendment is not a loose collection of separate clauses, but a compact description of a desirable political society.
>
> In other words, the amendment is not a casual array of clauses or high-minded principles, and it does not deed freedom of the press as a property right to journalists or any

---

[8]Schudson, *"The good citizen,"* pp. 73–77.
[9]Carey, *"A critical reader,"* p. 238.

particular group. On this reading, the First Amendment describes the public and the ground conditions of public debate rather than merely enumerating rights possessed by groups.

Public life, Carey contended, "stands for a form of politics in which, in Jefferson's phrase, 'We could all be participants in the government of our affairs.' Carey continued: "Only when we can speak and act as citizens—and have some promise that others will see, hear and remember what we say—will an interest in public life grow and persist."[10]

Earlier Carey wrote about the role of the press in public life:

A free press is a necessary condition of a free public life, but it is not the same thing as a free public life. If I am right in contending that we should value the press to the precise degree that it sustains public life, that it helps keep the conversation going among us, and that we devalue the press to the degree that it seeks to inform us and turn us into silent spectators, then there are two diremptions of the central meaning of the First Amendment against which we must be on guard. The first is the tendency of the press to treat us like a client, a group with childlike dependence and an eight-year-old mind incapable of functioning at all without our daily dose of the news....

Second, the press endangers us when it disarms us, when it convinces us that just by sitting at home watching the news or spending an hour with the newspaper, we are actually participating in the affairs that govern our lives.[11]

The views of Carey and Schudson are not necessarily mutually exclusive, and they clearly were not "debating" one another when they wrote. But their views do reflect two distinct understandings of what the First Amendment was intended to do and what is implied through it about the role of journalists in democracy. Both writers, it should be noted, argued that the First Amendment did not convey unlimited rights or any responsibilities directly on journalists. The phrase "and of the press" had little if anything to do with any institution; it was a right conferred on citizens. Schudson's position is that the amendment was virtually an afterthought, a function of the concept of federalism. Carey's position is that the liberty of the press was only one element in a "compact description of a desirable political society" rather than some sort of conferred property right.

Under either interpretation, professional journalists who don the armor of the phrase "and of the press" are obligated to construct their own meanings and frame their own responsibilities, and that has certainly come to pass. The amendment does not contemplate that *the press*, under whatever interpretation of the words, will be fair, accurate, honest or, of course, paid attention to—only that it must be free. Although it was originally written to

---

[10]Carey, "*A critical reader,*" p. 239.

[11]Carey, "*A critical reader,*" p. 220.

empower people rather than any institution, it has become, for the organized press, a license to self-define that is unique among U.S. institutions. Neither clergy nor bar nor medicine nor academe can claim, and have validated by the courts, more latitude in word and deed.

Of course, that enormous latitude is a mixed blessing. Alexis de Tocqueville recognized and sardonically reflected on the uniquely free status of America's press early in his writings about 19th century American democracy:

> I confess that I do not entertain that firm and complete attachment to the liberty of the press which is wont to be excited by things that are supremely good in their very nature. I approve of it from a consideration more of the evils it prevents than of the advantages that it ensures.[12]

Also recognizing the absolute necessity of that liberty, Touqueville said, "In this question ... there is no medium between servitude and license; in order to enjoy the inestimable benefits that the liberty of the press ensures, it is necessary to submit to the inevitable evils that it creates."[13]

So today's press, as it has come to be constituted, theoretically has a blank sheet of paper. It is free to form its own answer to the fundamental question put by Jay Rosen: "What are journalists for?" In his book by that name, Rosen, of New York University's Department of Journalism and Mass Communication, pointed out that the sheet of paper isn't exactly blank. It has more than 200 years of changing traditions that defined and redefined the organized press' role. From the 1920s on, Rosen wrote, the prevailing wisdom of the press has answered his two-pronged question ("Why do we need journalists? What do they stand for?) this way:

> Journalists ... give us timely information about matters of common importance; they entertain and enlighten us with compelling stories; they act as our surrogate or watchdog before the high and the mighty, asking sharp questions and demanding straight answers; they expose wrongdoing and the abuse of public trust; and they put before us a range of views, through opinion forums marked as such. What do journalists stand for?
>
> They uphold the public's right to know, a spirit of openness and honesty in the conduct of public business, the free flow of information and ideas, along with truthfulness, accuracy, balance, and fair play in the news. Beyond that, standing up for things is best left to others. Journalists do not join the parade because their job is to report on the parade.[14]

---

[12]Alexis de Tocqueville, *"Democracy in America."* New York: Vintage Classic, 1990, p. 184.

[13]Tocqueville, *"Democracy in America,"* p. 185.

[14]Jay Rosen, *"What are journalists for?"* New Haven, CT: Yale University Press, 1999, p. 281.

That conventional response to his query, Rosen said, has "helped create a strong institution—profitable, powerful, and, on the whole, dedicated to public service. The answer sketched above has served the press well." But, as he pointed out, the press itself isn't "well," nor is public life.[15]

So there is a problem that Rosen and others, including us as the authors of this book, see in future journalists remaining tied to that prevailing wisdom as a complete, eternal response. If, as James Carey argued, "we should value the press to the precise degree that it sustains public life, that it helps keep the conversation going among us, and (we should) devalue the press to the degree that it seeks to inform us and turn us into silent spectators,"[16] what culpability, and then responsibility, does the press have when that conversation of public life wanes and turns sour?

Journalists are not inextricably bound by the tradition of the last 80 years and are still free to self-define. Notice that the prevailing-wisdom response reflects journalists acting out of what Carey styled "a property right" deeded to them rather than out of a responsibility felt toward a broader "description of a desirable political society." Not being bound by those traditions, where do journalists turn to begin to construct a more active and robust self-definition?

For a start, we as journalists can use our understandings of our origins in the First Amendment to help think about the nature of that "desirable political society" and our role in it. To do so, we move into the early 20th century.

Suggestions for Additional Reading

Akhil Reed Amar, "*The Bill of Rights.*" New Haven, CT: Yale University Press, 1998.
James Carey, "*A critical reader.*" Minneapolis: University of Minnesota Press, 1997.

---

[15]Jay Rosen, "*What are journalists for?*," p. 281.

3

Conflicting Visions
of Democracy

We are not used to a complicated civilization, we don't know how to behave when personal contact and eternal authority have disappeared. There are no precedents to guide us, no wisdom that wasn't made for a simpler age.

We have changed our environment more quickly than we know how to change ourselves. … The modern man is not yet settled in his world. … It is strange to him, terrifying, alluring, and incomprehensibly big.
—Walter Lippmann, *"Drift and Mastery"*[1]

Steam has given us electricity and has made the nation a neighborhood. The electric wire, the iron pipe, the street railroad, the daily newspaper, the telephone, the lines of transcontinental traffic by rail and water … have made us all one body—socially, industrially, politically. … It is possible for all men to understand one another.
—William Allen White, *"The Old Order Changeth"*[2]

Almost a century ago, two thoughtful and renowned journalist-philosophers came to strikingly different conclusions about the nature of their society. Walter Lippmann, the sophisticated Easterner, member of journalism's elite and co-founder of the *New Republic,* and William Allen White, the plain-spoken Midwesterner and publisher of *The Emporia Gazette* in Kansas, both were reflecting on the social and political impact of the industrial

---

[1]Quoted in Michael J. Sandel, *"Democracy's discontent."* Cambridge, MA: Belknap Harvard, 1996. Pp. 205–206.

[2]Quoted in Sandel, *"Democracy's discontent,"* p. 206.

revolution, trying to sort out its meaning for them and for the future of the nation. Were their intellects with us in today's exponentially more complex, more intricately connected and yet more harrowingly disparate society, what might they conclude and what implications would they draw for their profession?

As postindustrial revolution momentum steadily accelerated over the next three decades after they wrote those words, many voices joined the debate, voices that worried about the impact of change on people, institutions and professions. That bibliography of social and political commentary is too long and too deep to try to catalogue here. For journalism, however, one voice dominated across all those decades: Lippmann's. His dreary analysis of democratic possibilities in the "modern" world and the role of journalism in democracy influenced generations of journalists whether or not they had ever heard of him or read a word he had written. Through the 1920s and into the 1930s in a series of works including *"The Phantom Public"* and *"Public Opinion"* Lippmann described a democratic society in which citizens were necessarily relegated to the role of spectator, so self-involved and disinterested that their role, at best, consisted of casting an occasional vote. That vote, he believed, would be totally based in self-interest, going to the "ins" if the voter was reasonably happy and to the "outs" if the voter was unhappy.

Ordinary citizens, Lippmann insisted, were simply incapable of any larger role. The world in which they lived (recall this was in the 1920s) was so complex and distant and the ordinary citizens in it so inept, bewildered, biased, frivolous and incurious that democracy was best left to experts and elites who could at least have access to and perhaps understand the complex world that was so far beyond the comprehension of ordinary people.

Lippmann's "democratic realist" critique did not go unchallenged. John Dewey, the foremost democratic philosopher of the time, responded to Lippmann's analysis in a series of essays and articles in a debate that is a landmark in democratic theory and journalism history. Lippmann and Dewey agreed on many things, including most of the causes and symptoms of the challenge that the industrial revolution presented to democratic norms and the severity of that challenge. Where they departed was on the matter of possible and appropriate responses. Lippmann contended that the unseen environment was so vast, entangling and complex that there was a need to interpose some form of expertness between the private citizen and the environment. Those disinterested experts should direct their opinions not to average citizens but to a governing elite, shielding unprepared citizens from the duty and rigor of decision making except for the casting of an occasional vote.

Many prophetic things were written by both men during their exchanges, but one of the most prescient statements came from Dewey. He countered Lippmann's dreary view of the public's potential with this warning: "The very ignorance, bias, frivolity, jealousy, and instability which are alleged to incapacitate" ordinary citizens from governing themselves, he wrote, make them even less able to passively submit to rule by a governing elite.[3]

LIPPMANN PREVAILS

Lippmann's views, however, prevailed for decades, embodied in the Progressive reform movement that swept through government, institutions and social establishments. Experts would take care of things; citizens merely need stand by and occasionally calculate how happy they were. What happened, however, is that the information developed and possessed by the experts became confused in their minds as superior knowledge, and superior knowledge became misunderstood to be exclusive wisdom. A huge disconnect developed between the governing elite and ordinary citizens.

Journalism, too, was swept up in the reform movement and its fascination with elitism. Lippmann concluded that because journalism had to cope with that unseen environment, journalistic efforts were largely wasted on ordinary citizens. Rather, he argued, journalism should serve the specialized class of administrators and experts. Journalists and the governing and leadership elites were best suited to debate about and decide what should happen. As insiders, they were far better prepared to know what to do for the rest of the people.

As is usually the case with philosophical debates, no clear "winner" emerged from the Lippmann–Dewey exchange. The world simply moved on, as did the journalists engaged in their relentless pursuit of daily events. Based on journalists' behavior, however, it was clear that Lippmann's views, consciously or not for journalists, were more compatible with what they actually did than were Dewey's views. Perhaps this was because Lippmann was a recognized and respected member of the journalism establishment, whereas Dewey was, at that time at least, "merely a philosopher" who only late in life would enter the journalistic trenches. Thus Dewey, at the time of the exchange with Lippmann, had little prospect of being persuasive to journalists who see trench life as a legitimizing principle. Perhaps it was because Lippmann viewed life through the same journalistic lens as they did and thus was predestined to not so much form the views of other journalists as to validate the ones already held and being acted on.

For journalism, the inevitable consequence of Lippmann prevailing was an almost total, and in most ways calculated, disconnect between journalists and ordinary people. Many journalists began to see themselves as part of the elite, which inevitably disconnected them from ordinary citizens. No surprise,

---

[3]Quoted in Robert B. Westbrook, "*John Dewey and American democracy.*" Ithaca, NY: Cornell University Press, 1991, p. 312.

then, that a tenet of the conservative political movement is antagonism toward what it views as an elitist liberal media. It may reflect the sound of Dewey's citizens unable to passively submit to the decision making of an isolated elite.

To be fair, it must also be said that Lippmann's persuasive writing about journalism greatly elevated journalistic standards. He used the ideal of objectivity as a platform for urging new levels of fairness and accuracy. In the spirit of the Progressive era's wide-ranging institutional reforms that urged professionalism in all governments and institutions, journalism was also reformed and "professionalized." In the middle years of the century, newspapers became less partisan, their employees better trained, their reporting more "objective" (if also more detached). Not all of the new emphasis on objectivity was driven by philosophy. Publishers began to realize that blatant partisanship was a limiting factor on financial success. Why automatically offend half the potential audience and risk half the advertising revenue when "going down the middle" could attract larger numbers of readers and advertisers? By the middle of the century, the U.S. model of journalism was not recognizable to most of the rest of the world where the partisan model prevailed and largely does to this day. Whether that new model best serves both journalism and democracy is still an open question, for its usefulness to citizens is limited by the notion of detachment that journalists assumed came with the notion of objectivity. As we shall see, objectivity and detachment are not the same thing.

Whatever the reasons why Lippmann's views prevailed, the middle decades of the 20th century—even well into the late 1980s—saw little change in basic journalistic practice or serious challenge to its premises. The objectives of journalism were to provide information and analysis of events, keep effective watch over the excesses of government and other institutions, and vigorously protect the First Amendment that makes those activities possible.

But the environment in which Dewey and Lippmann had debated was fundamentally changing through those decades. Perhaps the most profound change can be summed up in the word *privatization*. The word is used here not in the current political sense of moving tasks from government to the private sector but in the sociological sense of people becoming self-referential, that is, viewing events, circumstances and opportunities as intensely personal in nature. It is, broadly, what sociologist Robert Putnam identified as "a solitary quest for private goods" taking the place of "the shared pursuit of the public good."[4] Self-interest is hardly a new human characteristic nor a uniquely American one, but the natural element of self-interest was tempered in previous generations by other concerns and limitations, such as family in its broadest sense, the interdependent dynamic of the immediate geographic community to which people were bound, and even concerns about society as a whole.

---

[4]Putnam, *"Bowling alone,"* p. 403.

Self-interest slid easily into self-absorption as those tempering factors were undermined by physical and psychological mobility. From the telegraph to the Internet, from paved roads with horseless carriages to superhighways with SUVs, from cooperative work on farms to individual work cubicles in towering glass boxes, from dependence on local providers of food and clothing to ubiquitous access to giant shopping malls and distant catalogue and e-commerce retailers, the spaces and styles in which people could function worked their paling effect on the tempering factors of proximity, collective security and filial ties. Money being fully portable, relative prosperity was the enabling factor in all of those changes, providing independence from immediate and limiting circumstances. Although most people believe money cannot provide happiness, it can in fact leverage one out of an unhappy marriage, it can provide a separate home for aged parents, it can reduce one's dependence on and thus loyalty to a specific employer, and it can even buy access to the seats of power. Good economic times decrease individuals' reliance on others and on the traditional ties of society, making self-privatization both more attractive and more possible. It is significant that the trend toward privatization of life has accelerated during the last decade in which the nation has experienced the longest and deepest economic expansion in its history.

ANOTHER SET OF VIEWS

Given the extent and pace of the changes, it is small wonder that observers of public life such as Putnam and Schudson debated about and struggled to define the nature of community, the public, and public life as the 21st century opens. These new intellectual struggles are as important to journalists and to the future of journalism as were Lippmann's and Dewey's debates 70 years earlier. Like Lippmann and Dewey, Putnam and Schudson seem to agree about the nature of many of the changes. Where they depart most sharply is in the implications of the changes—what they portend for the future of society and democracy. Because the aim of this chapter is to begin to round out our self-definition of the role of journalism in democracy, it is helpful to explore in some detail these different interpretations of what the social changes mean.

The exploration begins with the concept of social capital, the idea that social interaction has value. Putnam described it this way:

> Just as a screwdriver (physical capital) or a college education (human capital) can increase productivity (both individual and collective), so too social contacts affect the productivity of individuals and groups. Whereas physical capital refers to physical objects and human capital refers to properties of individuals, social capital refers to

connections among individuals—social networks and the norms of reciprocity and trustworthiness that arise from them.[5]

Recall our fictional John and Mary. Social capital, like other kinds of capital, can be accrued, and it can be spent, even to the point of bankruptcy. Social capital, like other kinds of capital, also can be put to negative uses. The example Putnam used is Timothy McVeigh's bombing of the federal building in Oklahoma City: "McVeigh's network of friends, bound together by norms of reciprocity, enabled him to do what he could not have done alone."[6] The challenge, Putnam said, is to "ask how the positive consequences of social capital—mutual support, cooperation, trust, institutional effectiveness—can be maximized and the negative manifestations— sectarianism, ethnocentrism, corruption—minimized."[7] Is social capital real, that is, more than an interesting sociological concept? And if so, what practical implications does it have for journalists and for democracy?

Again, Putnam is instructive. In 1970, Italy's central government decided to reinvent local governments in each of its 20 regions. From the Alps in the north to the southern tip of the boot, these widely different regions were given the same form of government, the same resources, and the same rights and powers. Putnam and two associates, Robert Leonardi and Raffaella Y. Nanetti,[8] spent more than 20 years following the progress of the reform with the idea of identifying the conditions that create the social capital necessary for a society to be successful, that is, economically healthy, socially robust and educationally sound: in other words, the conditions for these new governmental institutions to succeed.

During this two-decade study, a long list of standard activities were tracked: voting, civic involvement through associations, newspaper reading, strength of political parties and other things that might be called an indication of civic-ness. Consistent methods were used to measure outcomes, such as economic well-being, the effectiveness of the local government and the presence or lack of corruption in government. At the end of 20 years, clear differences had emerged among the regions. Some were successful, some were not. Life in some was vibrant and peaceful; in others, it was dangerous and difficult. Geography played no determining role: The "good" and "bad" regions were scattered across the map. Neither was history a guide: Some that had been relatively successful before the change were no longer successful, and some that had been unsuccessful were now thriving.

Sifting through all of the factors, Putnam and his associates came on a startling fact: The two most consistent predictors of a region's success were

---

[5]Putnam, "*Bowling alone*," p. 19.

[6]Putnam, "*Bowling alone*," p. 21.

[7]Putnam, "*Bowling alone*," p. 22.

[8]Robert D. Putnam with Robert Leonardi and Raffaella Nanetti, "*Making democracy work: Civic traditions in modern Italy*." Princeton, NJ: Princeton University Press, 1993.

1) the associational involvement of citizens—their civic-ness and 2) news-paper reading. Social capital, then, is real and in its public manifestation as civic capital contributes heavily to the overall success of a society. So what are the implications for journalism and democracy of the trend toward self-privatization mentioned earlier? Again, there are no brightly limned answers; there are only ideas, and Putnam and Schudson offered differing views for our consideration as we think about the environment for 21st century public affairs reporting.

BOWLING ALONE

In 1995, Putnam published an essay, *Bowling Alone*, and in 2000 a book by the same name.[9] The bowling metaphor sprang from the fact that although more Americans than ever bowl for recreation, far fewer participate in bowling leagues. In the essay, which struck a chord nationally among people concerned about civic life, and in greater detail in the subsequent book, Putnam argued that civic life in this country is imperiled by people turning inward; that people's civic and personal well-being are threatened by a sharp decline in social capital.

If Putnam's well-researched description of a decline is correct, what difference does it make? Social capital, he argued, helps people translate aspirations into realities. These include allowing citizens to resolve collective problems more easily, greasing the wheels that allow communities to advance smoothly, and widening our awareness of the many ways in which our fates are linked. A paucity of social capital works against those desirable outcomes.

Putnam points out that today's civic malaise is not the culmination of a steady slide downward from some gilded age of civic-mindedness in America. The pendulum swings. More than a century ago, Alexis de Touqueville, reflecting on his visit to America in 1831 and 1832, wrote this:

> Americans of all ages, all conditions and all dispositions constantly form Associations ... of a thousand ... kinds, religious, moral, serious, futile, general or restricted, enormous or diminutive. The Americans make associations to give entertainments, to found seminaries, to build inns, to construct churches, to diffuse books, to send missionaries to the antipodes; in this manner they found hospitals, prisons, schools.... If it is predisposed to inculcate some truth or to foster some feeling by encouragement of a great example, they found a society.[10]

When Tocqueville wrote this, America was still largely an agrarian, small-town society. The industrial revolution was only dawning. Near the

---

[9]Putnam, "*Bowling alone*," and Bowling alone: America's declining social capital, *Journal of Democracy*, 6:1, (1995), p. 66.

[10]Tocqueville, "*Democracy in America*," p. 106.

end of the century, the nation having passed through the trauma of the Civil War, things were changing rapidly. The industrial revolution was in full explosion; a wave of immigration from Europe and the job-related migration of Americans were building huge cities and beginning to empty the rural landscape. The realities of the industrial revolution—the need for workers, the emergence of an elite capitalist society, the regular boom-and-bust of a maturing but still adolescent national economy—created a set of social problems to which the old, localized associations could not respond effectively. By the end of the 19th century, the rules of social capital (although the term had not yet been coined) needed rewriting because its demographic and geographic foundations had shifted.

They received that rewriting during the Progressive era. For good or ill, and there was plenty of both, the Progressive (and Lippmannesque) idea that coping with the new social problems required a level of expertness and top-down management took strong hold. Associational life in America, within only a few decades, was revolutionized. Between 1871 and 1920, Putnam pointed out, more than 60 permanent national associations were formed: civic clubs such as Lions and Rotary, labor unions such as the Longshoremen and Electrical Workers, service groups such as the American Red Cross and League of Women Voters, fraternal groups such as the Loyal Order of Moose and Shriners, activity-based groups such as the American Bowling Congress and the Audubon Society and the National Rifle Association, and even the second iteration of the Ku Klux Klan and the new American Civil Liberties Union, the Boy Scouts and Girl Scouts, Big Sisters and the Sons of Italy.

Almost suddenly, the country was awash in affinity groups aimed not at building a seminary or giving an entertainment as Tocqueville found things, but at affecting social, economic and political life in a much broader and more profound way. The surge continued well into the 20th century, survived (and undoubtedly helped sustain the nation through) two world wars, and peaked shortly after World War II. But even more suddenly than it had risen, the tide began to recede.

Putnam, who believed the fabric of American community life began to unravel in the 1960s and accelerated in the 1980s and 1990s, searched for the reasons behind this decline.[11] He used the metaphor of a detective working through a long list of suspects, eliminating some from the usual list (mobility, two-career families, disruption of marriage and family ties are among those discounted) and indicting others (television, pressures of work in the new economy, urban and suburban sprawl). But for Putnam, the largest contributor is simply generational change. He pointed out that the "long civic generation," people born between 1910 and 1940 and affected by the cata-

---

[11]Putnam, *"Bowling alone,"* pp. 184–188.

clysmic events of the first half of the century such as the Great Depression and the world wars, are now at or beyond retirement. They are being replaced by two generations of people who are vastly different, the baby boomers (born between 1946 and 1964), now in mid-life, and the Generation Xers (born between 1965 and 1980), now reaching maturity. The boomers are substantially less engaged in civic affairs than their parents, and the Xers are even less so. Documenting those facts is one thing; ascribing a reason for the difference is quite another. For whatever reasons, those two generations have turned increasingly inward and are more materialistic and far less likely to engage in more than transient, temporary organizational activities.

As culprits, in addition to generational change, Putnam settled on television, sprawl and work regimes. Has life been simply too kind to those privatized generations? One can argue that advances in medicine, a generally good economy, ready access to higher levels of education, and the lack of a consuming national crisis have left those generations free to privatize their lives and ambitions. But why are they not happy about that? Putnam pointed out that each of the two latest generations has succeedingly higher rates of suicide and depression than its forebearers.

What's missing here? And what are the answers? Will the pendulum swing back by itself or will some new and perhaps very different national crisis have to occur for the civic malaise to ease? Certainly in the weeks immediately after the terrorist attacks of Sept. 11, 2001 there was a surge of patriotism and people seemed more inclined to work together and worry about things such as social capital and the benefits of cooperation. It is yet too early to know if the events will have a lasting effect, so people still face the question of whether a return to a rich associational life is crucial for a revival of civic life. And if so, what obligation, if any, do journalists have to help in that revival?

THE GOOD CITIZEN

Although Schudson might not have said to Putnam and his co-worriers, "Hey, chill out," he did counter, in *"The Good Citizen,"* that "Citizenship in the United States has not disappeared. It has not even declined. It has, inevitably, changed."[12]

The Progressive era ideal of the "informed citizen" simply doesn't apply in today's world, Schudson argued, nor should people yearn for a revival of it as the only cure for what seems to be civic malaise. The informed citizen model has been replaced by the "monitorial" citizen, a quite different sort of being, Schudson argued.[13] This proposition, which we explore in detail shortly, is important for journalists because for 80 years or more, journal-

---

[12]Schudson, *"The good citizen,"* p. 294.

[13]Schudson, *"The good citizen,"* pp. 294–314.

ism, particularly public affairs journalism, has been based on the informed citizen model. The job of journalists, the theory goes, is to provide detailed information about public affairs. This information will be eagerly sought and absorbed and analyzed by citizens who will then know what, if anything, to do with it. They may or may not make their desires known at polling places, in public meetings, in political conversations and letters to the editor. Underlying the notion of the informed citizen is that the citizen operates out of some sense of the public good as well as a sense of private good.

What they do or not do with information, the informed citizen model declares, need not be the concern of the journalists who provide the information. For journalists operating as detached providers of information, the task ends there. We tell the news; it is not our affair what they choose to do with it.

If, however, the informed citizen model has been replaced by some other model, does that change journalism's task? How? Students of democracy and journalism would be well-served to make both Putnam's *"Bowling Alone"* and Schudson's *"The Good Citizen"* primary reading. In contrast to the dense philosophizing of Lippmann and Dewey, they are accessible and well-documented.

In Schudson's view, American citizenship (and thus American civic capital) has evolved in stages. In pre-constitutional colonial America, the model was one of deference to the authority of elites, a more or less unavoidable state of affairs. What Schudson called "the constitutional moment" challenged that status quo and set up, for the first half of the 19th century, a period in which political parties dominated public life. The industrial revolution challenged the ability of parties to maintain their hold on masses of people, and the period of 1865 to 1920 gave rise to the Progressive era in which people began to relate more to issues and principles than to specific parties. The surge in associations that Putnam chronicled both reflected and fed this change.

It is at this point that Schudson's analysis and that of Putnam begin to diverge. Putnam spotted in the post-World War II years a weakening in the associational society as the beginning of a decline in civic-ness and loss of civic capital. Schudson argued that the weakening of associational ties was not necessarily a decline but simply a change. Measuring citizenship by the ruler of associational activity may not be the right or only way to define progress or decline. In fact, he said, "The decline in organizational solidarity ... is also the flip side of a rise in individual freedom, which is truly a gain."[14]

In Schudson's analysis, the primary shift after World War II was a revolution in individual rights:

> A growing inclination of people and organized groups to define politics in terms of rights, a growing willingness of the federal government to enforce individuals' claims

---

[14]Schudson, *"The good citizen,"* p. 307.

to constitutional rights, and a widening of the domain of 'politics' propelled by rights-consciousness. Both the nationalization of politics and the 'rights revolution' have been encouraged by, and further encouraged, the privatization of social life. This tripod of mutually reinforcing social forces—the expansion of government, the proliferation of rights, and the intensification of private social life—defines American political experience at the end of the twentieth century. It provides the framework in which a new mode 'rights-regarding' citizen is ascendant.[15]

Schudson's use of the word "ascendant" is significant, for he argued that none of the previous models of citizenship has been replaced. Vestiges of all of them survive, even the colonial model of deference to authority, and help form the foundation of today's version of citizenship.

The pressures of modern life, the rights revolution and the privatization of social life do not necessarily spell doom for civic life, Schudson contended, but a new model is needed. He described that new model as a monitorial obligation in which citizens know enough to participate intelligently in government affairs. Monitorial citizens, in comparison to informed citizens, scan (rather than read) the informational environment so that they can be alerted to actions affecting the wide variety of issues meaningful to them. Thus alerted to a threat or an opportunity, they form floating coalitions, temporary and often intense, to deal with it. In the America of Tocqueville and later in Putnam's "long civic generation" associations were more or less permanent and might deal with a variety of issues. The floating coalitions of Schudson's model dissolve when the problem goes away.

"Walter Lippmann was right," Schudson contended. "If democracy requires omnicompetence and omniscience from its citizens, it is a lost cause."[16] But, he argued, the monitorial citizen may provide an answer to that dilemma. "The monitorial citizen engages in environmental surveillance rather than information-gathering…. The monitorial citizen is not an absentee citizen but watchful, even while he or she is doing something else"[17] in their privatized lives. This is not without its dangers, Schudson conceded. "How much of the obligation to be knowledgeable about politics can people relinquish without doing violence to their democratic souls? There is surely some line of willful ignorance that, once crossed, crosses out democracy itself."[18]

TRYING TO MAKE SOME SENSE

What does all that mean for public affairs journalism? Does it matter whether Schudson or Putnam (or someone else, for that matter) has the most

---

[15]Schudson, *"The good citizen,"* p. 242.

[16]Schudson, *"The good citizen,"* p. 310.

[17]Schudson, *"The good citizen,"* p. 311.

[18]Schudson, *"The good citizen,"* p. 311.

From one perspective, this indeterminacy is fortunate because a major goal of this book is to foster discussion and debate—perhaps even have some influence—on the course of this evolution in the new media setting. Although no one knows exactly what will emerge in the next decade or two, individuals can have some influence on what does emerge because the creative and entrepreneurial spirit of journalists, singly and in various combinations, has been a potent force in the evolution of American journalism during the past two centuries.

An important point to keep in mind is that the shifting nature of journalism over the 19th and 20th centuries and now in the opening decade of the 21st century basically has been evolutionary rather than characterized by abrupt shifts at specific historical junctures. This is the case because the changes in journalism—and, more broadly, the changes in mass communication—over these centuries result from the confluence of three major factors:[2]

- new developments in technology.
- changes in the undergirding social conditions.
- and creative and entrepreneurial impulses.

In the 1830s, when mass communication began with the penny press, the convergence of influences producing this phenomenon was the new technology of steam-driven printing presses capable of producing large numbers of copies of newspapers; widespread literacy as the supporting social condition; and a key entrepreneur, Benjamin Day, who launched the *New York Sun*. But Day alone did not create the style and the norms for this new journalism. Those were the product of numerous editors and working journalists, a few well known to us, such as James Gordon Bennett and Horace Greeley, but most anonymous.

THIRTY-YEAR VANTAGE POINTS

Any activity such as journalism that results from the creative and intellectual efforts of hundreds of different organizations geographically scattered across many cities will be characterized largely by evolution. It is difficult, if not impossible, to perceive distinct changes from day to day or even from month to month. But as these shifts and changes accumulate over time, they do become apparent. An optimum strategy for observing the evolution of American journalism from the days of the penny press to the present is to dip into this historical stream at intervals of 30 years. Not only is three decades a sufficiently broad interval of time to make changes in the nature of

---

[2]Melvin DeFleur and Sandra Ball-Rokeach, *"Theories of mass communication,"* 4th edition. New York: Longman, 1982. Chapter 2 discusses the first two of these factors, technology and driving social conditions.

journalism readily apparent, an interval of three decades also means that a new generation has come onto the scene and made its mark. Those persons who would have been novices at one point in time will have become, 30 years later, the cadre of experienced journalists and editors occupying most of the key positions in news organizations. Today's 22-year-old graduating with a bachelor's degree in journalism may well be, by age 52, the managing editor or even editor of a daily newspaper—or occupying a similar high level position in other news media. No generation is a perfect clone of its predecessor. Each generation brings change and by the time that 30 years have passed, each new generation is likely to have made its mark on the practice of journalism.

This situation is not unique to journalism. Arthur M. Schlesinger Jr. noted the utility that the concept of generation has generally for historical analysis and explanations of change:

> In traditional societies, where change was imperceptible and each generation lives as its parents and grandparents had lived before it, the passage of generations made little difference. But, with the acceleration in the velocity of history, new generations began to undergo novel experiences and thereby to achieve distinctive outlooks.[3]

He also noted the influence of Auguste Comte—in Schlesinger's view, the first person to recognize the historical significance of generations—on John Stuart Mill who asserted that historical change should be measured by "intervals of one generation, during which a new set of human beings have been educated, have grown up from childhood, and taken possession of society."[4] Although both Jose Ortega y Gasset[5] and Karl Mannheim[6] identified a generation's lifetime as 30 years—an interval also used by Schlesinger to analyze the 20th century political history of the United States as alternating cycles in the dominance of public purpose and private interest—Ortega y Gasset urged caution:

> There is no arithmetical inevitability in the generational sequence. A generation is a rough, not an exact, unit; almost a metaphor.[7]

This idea of generations, in particular generational replacement, also has been used to explain fundamental changes in public opinion over time. Few

---

[3]Arthur M. Schlesinger Jr., *"The cycles of American history."* p. 29. Boston: Houghton Mifflin, 1986.

[4]John Stuart Mill quoted in Schlesinger, *"The cycles of American history,"* p. 29.

[5]Jose Ortega y Gasset, *"The modern theme,"* The concept of the generation. New York, 1961, pp. 14–15.

[6]Karl Mannheim, *"Essays on the sociology of knowledge,"* The problem of generations. London, 1952, p. 290.

[7]Ortega y Gasset quoted in Schlesinger, *"The cycles of American history,"* p. 30.

people radically shift their opinions about the issues of the times, but over time, one generation of opinion holders is replaced by a new generation with new perspectives and opinions on the issues of the day. Journalist Samuel Lubell attributed the long-running success of the Democratic Party in the 1930s and 1940s to the generations of voters that came of age during the Great Depression.[8] Later generations shifted the tide to the Republican Party. As an international example, the strongest support for social welfare policies in both the United States and western Europe is found among the generations that attained adulthood after these programs were already in place in the societies in which they grew up. There are many other examples of differences between generations and their differing approach to the times.[9]

Without delving too deeply into the historical details, think about a historical timeline of American journalism from the 1830s to the present. Thirty years after the appearance of the penny press is the time of the Civil War with news stories frequently constructed in inverted pyramids and modeled on the principle of objectivity. Thirty years later is the end of the 19th century and a time when the yellow journalism of William Randolph Hearst and Joseph Pulitzer epitomized much of mainstream journalism. Next are the 1920s and the perceived need in the complex aftermath of World War I to offer news analysis as well as spot news about the events of the day. By the mid-20th century, television news was a major part of mass communication and a continuing influence on the style of journalism.

The final decades of the 20th century are the ones that define for many journalists, including us as the authors of this book, significant portions of their professional careers. Contemporary journalism is delivered through far more channels than it was when we were college undergraduates in journalism. Daily newspapers and both network and local television still command significant, though shrinking, audiences.[10] Now these media share the public arena with a multitude of cable news channels, online newspapers and a variety of other news sources.

CHANGING STYLES OF NEWS

Much more has changed than the variety of media that deliver the news. The style of that news also has changed significantly. A succinct portrait of this

---

[8] Samuel Lubell, *"The future of American politics."* New York, 1952.

[9] See, for example, Michael X. Delli Carpini, *"Stability and change in American politics: The coming of age of the generation of the 1960s."* New York: New York University Press, 1986. Also see M. Kent Jennings and Richard D. Niemi, *"Generations and politics: A panel study of young adults and their parents."* Princeton, NJ: Princeton University Press, 1981.

[10] Thomas Patterson, *"Doing well and doing good: How soft news and critical journalism are shrinking the new audience and weakening democracy—and what news outlets can do about it."* Cambridge, MA: Harvard University, Joan Shorenstein Center on the Press, Politics and Public Policy, 2000.

evolutionary pattern in contemporary journalism during the final decades of the 20th century is found in Thomas Patterson's *"Out of Order,"* an analysis of how the news media covered our presidential elections from 1960 to 1992.[11] Again, an interval of approximately 30 years proves a useful vantage point for sketching these changes.

In 1960, an interpretative framework—rather than the more traditional descriptive framework used to report the presidential election—was found in only a small fraction of the news stories on the front page of the *New York Times*. By 1972, there was parity between the two styles of election reporting; in the 1988 and 1992 elections, interpretative stories dominated the front page of the *New York Times* by a ratio of 4-to-1. Over a period of approximately 30 years, the preferred style for reporting the presidential election had turned upside down.

By 1960 there already was an emphasis on politics as a game in which reporting a candidate's strategy for winning and conjuring with such things as "who won the day" and "who is ahead by how much" were key elements. That is, the thrust of the reportage was on the campaign as a contest between parties and politicians rather than on the election as a method for the public to make a decision about its future. In that 1960 election, the split between reporting on the game and reporting on the issues was close to 50-50. This already was very different from elections in earlier periods, but that 50-50 split was just the baseline for major changes appearing in the 1972 and 1976 elections. By 1972, reporting on the game prevailed by about 2-to-1. By 1976, the ratio of game coverage to issue coverage had reached a new plateau of about 4-to-1.

Among the most powerful influences driving the startling shift to a 4-1 ratio of strategic, insider reporting over issues reporting was Theodore H. White. Starting in 1960, White, a veteran reporter, produced a best-selling series of quadrennial books, *"The Making of the President."* Remarkable in their detailed reporting from inside the presidential campaigns, the books set a new standard for depth and insight into the strategic and human calculations that elected presidents.

White was writing history, but the seemingly authenticating details that his books contained proved irresistible to the political press; never mind that they were reported months after the votes were cast. The Associated Press, for instance, messaged its political reporters, "When Teddy White's book comes out, there shouldn't be a single story in that book that we haven't reported ourselves." And A. M. Rosenthal, managing editor of the *New York Times*, instructed his staff, "We aren't going to wait until a year after the election to read in Teddy White's book what we should have reported ourselves."[12]

---

[11]Thomas Patterson, *"Out of order."* New York: Random House Vintage Books, 1993.

[12]Quoted in Joyce Hoffman, *"Theodore H. White and journalism as an illusion."* Columbia: University of Missouri Press, 1995, p. 173.

The impact of such commands was to drive political reporting further and further inside the campaigns and away from issue coverage. The narrative illusion was if you can report what's in the candidate's stomach, that is, if you know what he had for breakfast, then you surely must also know what's in his head and heart. What journalists failed to recognize was that White's books were not helpful to the public in terms of picking a leader, for the rich details they contained were published months after the votes were cast. They were conceived and executed as history, not contemporary journalism. Nevertheless, the hunger for glimpses into the inner circles and thoughts of the campaigns moved political reporting ever further from anything that could be useful, or even very interesting, to average voters.

Even White himself came to regret his reportorial invention. "It's appalling what we've done," White said during the 1972 campaign, the fourth of the five he chronicled. "All of us are observing him (the candidate), taking notes like mad, getting all the little details. Which I think I invented as a method of reporting and which I now sincerely regret. If you write about this, say that I sincerely regret it. Who gives a … if the guy had milk and Total for breakfast?"[13]

Not surprisingly, as shifts occurred among the aspects of the campaign that were emphasized in news reports, the journalist's voice also became more prominent in setting the tone of election reports. Back in 1960, the candidates themselves and partisan participants in the election set the tone in two-thirds of the stories. Praise for a candidate came from his supporters, attacks and criticism from his opponent and the opponent's supporters. By the 1972 presidential election, journalists were setting the tone of most articles.

Looking more closely at the nature of that tone reveals another pattern that turned upside down across those nine elections from 1960 to 1992; good news versus bad news. Back in 1960, the ratio of good news to bad news was about 3-to-1. This ratio seesawed up and down over the next four elections but in 1980 moved to a new plateau where the ratio of good news to bad news was 2-to-3, another 30-year reversal in the prevailing style of political reporting. This 30-year trend is graphically illustrated by the titles on *Time* magazine's cover stories. In 1960, they were simply "Candidate Kennedy" and "Candidate Nixon." In 1992, they included "Nobody's Perfect: The Doubts About Ross Perot" and "Waiting for Perot: He's Leading in the Polls, But Can He Lead the Nation?." Bush's cover story was "The Fight of His Life" and Clinton's cover stories included "Why Voters Don't Trust Clinton" and "Is Bill Clinton for Real?."

In sum, the pattern of presidential election coverage that evolved bit by bit from 1960 to 1992 resulted in a fundamentally different election journalism. In 1960, journalists described the campaign, issue coverage was prior-

---

[13]Timothy Crouse, *"The boys on the bus."* New York: Ballentine Books, 1974, p. 37.

ity, partisans set the tone of the coverage, and good news prevailed over bad news. Thirty years later, journalists interpreted the campaign, game coverage was the priority, the tone of the coverage was set by journalists, and bad news prevailed over good news.

The sequence of these steps in the evolution of a new style of political reporting is diagrammed in Fig. 4.1, where the Xs mark elections with significant increases over past journalistic practice. This stair-step pattern is a succinct portrait of shifting professional perspectives, the evolution of a new set of "cookie cutters" that shape contemporary political journalism.

Beyond political journalism and presidential elections, there are numerous other cookie cutters used to shape the daily news, many with long histories of use. Noting the repetition of master narratives—even rather specific stories—over and over through the years, even centuries, Robert Darnton metaphorically summarized his time as a journalist:

> We simply drew on the traditional repertory of genres. It was like making cookies
> from an antique cookie cutter.[14]

Among the most ancient sets of journalistic cookie cutters are political, financial and sexual scandals, cookie cutters extensively employed in the final decade of the 20th century whose historical origins are in the broadside ballads, news books and French canards of the 16th and 17th century.[15]

BAD NEWS					**X**				
CAMPAIGN CONTROVERSIES				**X**					
JOURNALISTIC VOICE			**X**	**X**			→	→	
THE GAME			**X**	**X**					
INTERPRETATION	→	→	→	**X**				**X**	
	1960	1964	1968	1972	1976	1980	1984	1988	1992

FIG. 4.1 The evolution of new "cookie cutters" for political news. The Xs mark the year of years when news stories on the presidential election reflected a significant increase, a sizeable jump, in this style of reporting. The → indicate a slowly rising trend. Prepared by Maxwell McCombs from data presented in Patterson, *"Out of Order."*

---

[14]Robert Darnton, Writing news and telling stories, *Daedalus*, 104 (1975), p. 189.

[15]Mitchell Stephens, *"A history of news: From the drum to the satellite."* New York: Viking, 1988.

In reporting the news of the moment, journalists depend for the most part on a set of standard conventions about how a news story should be written. Some of these are very ancient, some very recent. The mix of cookie cutters in common use is constantly evolving, and an interval of 30 years is a useful vantage point for observing what has changed and what has remained constant in reporting the news.

Journalism changed in the closing decades of the 20th century, in particular adding a strong interpretive element to the reporting of public affairs in general, not just political campaigns.[16] Undoubtedly, journalism will change again during the opening decades of this century. Part of the change will result from the tremendous changes in communication technology and its diffusion among the public. In *"Mediamorphosis: Understanding New Media,"* Roger Fidler cited Paul Saffo, a director at the Institute for the Future in Menlo Park, Calif., who "posits that the amount of time required for new ideas to fully seep into a culture has consistently averaged about three decades for at least the past five centuries. He calls this the 30-year rule."[17]

EVOLUTION OF JOURNALISM

Our purpose here is not to present a history of journalism using intervals of 30 years or any other vantage point. That is a massive undertaking for another book. Rather, our purpose is to make the point that the nature of journalism constantly evolves in response to the social, technological and creative environment in which people work. Furthermore, the defining characteristics of this evolution need to be made explicit and the subject of intense scrutiny and debate, especially in this time when a rapidly changing technological environment arguably offers more options than at any time in the past. Not all of these options—or even the current emphases of news, however long they last—are beneficial ones for society or for journalism. It is especially important to note "wrong turns" along the way or the failure to shed some bad habits. And there is the need to more explicitly guide this evolutionary pattern of the new journalism, not a new style of newspaper journalism or broadcast journalism, but rather a journalism resulting from the convergence of many media on the contemporary stage.

---

[16]For another important perspective on the interpretative role of journalism based on detailed interviews with a large, representative sample of U.S. journalists, see David H. Weaver and G. Cleveland Wilhoit, *"The American journalist in the 1990s: U.S. news people at the end of an era."* Mahwah, NJ: Lawrence Erlbaum Associates, 1996, Chapter 4.

[17]Roger Fidler, *"Mediamorphosis: Understanding new media."* Thousand Oaks, CA: Pine Forge Press, 1997, p. 8, who cites Paul Saffo and the 30-year rule, Design World, 24, (1992), p. 18.

Suggestions for Additional Reading

Thomas Patterson, *"Out of order."* New York: Random House Vintage Books, 1993.

Mitchell Stephens, *"A history of news: From the drum to the satellite."* New York: Viking, 1988.

CHAPTER

5

What the Public
Needs To Know

The public, in whose name all journalists ply their trade, is best understood as an achievement of good journalism—its intended outcome rather than its assumed audience.

—Jay Rosen, *"What Are Journalists For?"*[1]

Prominent in the rhetoric of journalism is the phrase "what the public needs to know." But do the traditional criteria of newsworthiness—everyone can recite the list—really specify the kinds of information that individuals need to know to function as citizens? How much of the daily news produced by your favorite newspaper or television news program has any practical value for the ordinary citizen in the street? Or is the phrase "what the public needs to know" only a rationalization, a reflexive defense of the routines and traditions that govern how journalism does its day-to-day business? Or worse, is this an arrogant attempt by journalists to define for citizens what should be, from the journalists' insider perspective, necessary knowledge and interest?

Far more topics compete for attention than any news organization possibly can cover, and most public affairs topics are too complex and slow-moving for a simple stenographic approach to reporting. Hard decisions have to be made about which stories to cover and how to write them. Are journalists truly guided by a critically honed sense of what the public needs to know? Look at the stories on the front page of this morning's

---

[1]Jay Rosen, *"What are journalists for?,"* p. 75.

newspaper and scan the lead items on the television newscast. Are these the things ordinary citizens need to know? Would they likely attract the attention of Schudson's monitorial citizens who are scanning the information environment for useful information that can affect their lives? How can an ordinary citizen use this information? Are the news media effective public communicators?

George Bernard Shaw once remarked that every profession is a conspiracy against the public. By a conspiracy he meant that every profession, such as the law, accounting and journalism, creates grounds rules and traditions to govern its behavior with little explicit regard to the needs or convenience of the public whom the profession ostensibly serves. On rare occasion, prominent journalists do reflect on their professional decisions about which topics to include in the daily news and how to frame those topics, that set of decisions that define the daily agenda of news offered to the public. James Fallows wrote a book, *"Breaking the News: How the Media Undermine Democracy,"* which dealt harshly with the traditional media's choices. And an executive producer of *"Nightline"* once asked in a moment of doubt, "Who are we to think we should set an agenda for the nation? What made us any smarter than the next guy?"[2]

Before pursuing the details of these questions about the quality of the media agenda, we consider in some detail that powerful phrase about the role of the media, "set an agenda for the nation."

AGENDA-SETTING ROLE OF THE NEWS MEDIA

The power of the news media to set the nation's agenda, to focus public attention on a few key public issues, is an immense and well-documented influence. Not only do people acquire factual information about public affairs from the news media, readers and viewers also learn how much importance to attach to a topic on the basis of the emphasis placed on it in the news. Newspapers provide a host of cues about the salience of the topics in the daily news—lead story on Page 1, other front page display, large headlines, and length, for example. Television news also offers numerous cues about salience including placement as the opening story on the newscast, length of time devoted to the story, and promotional emphasis put on it. These cues repeated day after day communicate the importance that journalists attach to each topic. In other words, the news media set the agenda for the public's attention to a small group of issues.

Because of this unavoidable influence on the public mind, the values journalists apply in their decision-making process become crucial. When

---

[2]Tom Bettag, What's news? Evolving definitions of news, *Harvard International Journal of Press/Politics*, 5:3 (2000), p. 105.

the traditional news values are applied, one sort of influence occurs. When, however, other values intervene in the process, such as anxiety over ratings or confusing entertainment with substance, quite another sort of influence happens.

The principal outlines of the media's agenda influence were sketched by Walter Lippmann in his 1922 classic, "*Public Opinion*," which began with a chapter titled "The World Outside and the Pictures in Our Heads." As Lippmann noted, the news media are a primary source of those pictures in our heads about the larger world of public affairs, a world that for most citizens is "out of reach, out of sight, out of mind."[3] What we know about the larger world is largely based on what the media decide to tell us. More specifically, the result of this mediated view of the world is that elements prominent on the media agenda become prominent in the public mind.

Social scientists examining this agenda-setting influence of the news media on the public usually have focused on public issues. The agenda of a news organization is its pattern of coverage on public issues over some period of time—a week, a month, an entire year. Over this period of time, whatever it might be, a few issues are emphasized, some receive light coverage, and many are seldom or never mentioned. It should be noted that the use of term *agenda* here is purely descriptive. There is no pejorative implication that a news organization "has an agenda" in the sense of specific policy outcomes. The media agenda presented to the public results from countless day-to-day decisions by many different journalists and their supervisors about the relative importance of the news of the moment, or, in some unfortunate cases, their focus on values other than importance. Some partisan or interest groups attempt to tease out a journalistic political agenda. Most fail to make a persuasive case because of two factors: Their own starting assumptions bias their analyses, and for most general-interest media, there simply is no specific political or ideological agenda.

The public agenda—the focus of public attention—can be assessed by public opinion polls asking the widely used Gallup Poll question, "What is the most important problem facing this country today?" The American public's responses to this question over the past half century provide a fascinating portrait of our political and civic history and yield significant evidence of the agenda-setting role of the news media. For example, when Chapel Hill, N. C. voters were asked to name the most important issues of the day —in the very first empirical study of this agenda-setting influence—their responses closely reflected the pattern of news coverage during the previous month in the mix of newspapers, network television news and news magazines available to them.[4] Since that initial study during the 1968 presidential

---

[3]Walter Lippmann, "*Public opinion*." New York: Macmillan, 1922, p. 29.

[4]Maxwell McCombs and Donald Shaw, The agenda-setting function of mass media, *Public Opinion Quarterly*, 36 (1972), 176–187.

election, hundreds of published studies worldwide have documented this influence of the news media on what people think is important.

To summarize the extent of this influence—and to facilitate comparisons from one setting to another—social scientists frequently calculate the correlation between the ranking of issues on the media agenda and the ranking accorded those same issues on the subsequent public agenda. This quantitative measure provides a substantial degree of precision for those comparisons much as a thermometer's precise numbers are better than simply saying it seems cooler today than it was yesterday. The possible range of scores for this correlation statistic is from a high of +1, perfect agreement between the media and the public on the ranking of the issues; down to 0, no agreement whatsoever about the rank ordering of the issues; and on to a low of –1, a perfectly inverse relationship between the ranks of the issues on the two agendas. The vast majority of comparisons between how issues are ranked on the media agenda—a measure of the relative emphasis by the media on these issues—and how the public ranks the importance of these issues yield correlations of +.50 or better.[5] That is a substantial degree of influence.

The initial study of the agenda-setting influence of the news media in Chapel Hill examined a month during the 1968 presidential election. Others have examined much longer periods of time and found similar evidence of strong agenda-setting effects among the public. A look at the entire decade of the 1960s found a substantial correlation (+.78) between the patterns of coverage in news magazines and the trends in public opinion reflected by responses to the Gallup Poll's question about the most important problem facing the country.[6] A look at a single issue, civil rights, over a crucial 23-year period, 1954 to 1976, found a similar match (+.71) between public concern about this issue and the pattern of rising and falling front page news in the *New York Times* during each preceding month.[7] A similar analysis of 11 different individual issues during the 1980s found a median correlation of +.45 in the comparison of Gallup Polls and a broad sample of newspapers, television news and news magazines. All of the comparisons were positive except for morality—a topic seldom discussed in the news.[8]

Nor are agenda-setting effects limited to the agenda of national issues. In Louisville, a comparison of public concern about eight local issues with coverage in the *Louisville Times* across 8 years also yielded a substantial

[5]Wayne Wanta and Salma Ghanem, Effects of agenda-setting. In *"Meta-analyses of media effects,"* Jennings Bryant and Rodney Carveth,(Eds.). Mahwah, NJ: Lawrence Erlbaum Associates, forthcoming.

[6]Ray Funkhouser, The issues of the sixties, *Public Opinion Quarterly*, 37 (1973), 62–75.

[7]James Winter and Chaim Eyal, Agenda setting for the civil rights issue, *Public Opinion Quarterly*, 45 (1981), 376–383.

[8]Howard Eaton Jr., Agenda setting with bi-weekly data on content of three national media, *Journalism Quarterly*, 66 (1989), 942–948.

match (+.65).[9] The news media have a substantial influence on the content of the public agenda, and the phrase "setting the agenda" has become commonplace in discussions of journalism and public opinion.

INFLUENCING THE PICTURES IN OUR HEADS

The agenda-setting influence of the news media is not limited to this initial step of focusing public attention on a particular topic. The media also influence the next step in the communication process; our understanding and perspective on the topics in the news. If you think about the agenda in abstract terms, the potential for a broader view of media influence on public opinion becomes very clear. In the abstract, the items that define the agenda are *objects*. For all the agendas we have discussed, the objects are public issues, but they could be other items or topics such as the agenda of political candidates during the presidential primaries. The objects are the things on which the attention of the media and, subsequently the public, are focused.

In turn, each of these objects has numerous *attributes*, those characteristics and traits that describe the object. For each object there also is an agenda of attributes because when the media and the public think and talk about an object, some attributes are emphasized, others are given less attention, and many receive no attention at all. This agenda of attributes is another aspect of the agenda-setting role of the news media.

To borrow Lippmann's phrase, "the pictures in our heads," the agenda of issues or other objects presented by the news media influence what the pictures in our heads are about. The agenda of attributes presented for each of these issues, public figures or other objects literally influences the pictures themselves that we hold in mind.

Images held by the public of political candidates and other public figures are the most obvious examples of attribute agenda setting by the news media. During the 1976 presidential primaries, the descriptions by Democrat voters in upstate New York of their party's contenders for the nomination already showed considerable correspondence (+.64) in early February with the media's presentation of these men. By late March, the match had increased to +.83. Voters not only learned the media's agenda of attributes; with additional exposure to the news, they learned it even better.[10]

In the national contest that year between incumbent President Jerry Ford and challenger Jimmy Carter, the median correlation across the entire election year between the Chicago *Tribune*'s agenda of attributes and the pictures of these two men in the minds of Chicago-area voters was

---

[9]Kim Smith, Newspaper coverage and public concern about community issues, *Journalism Monographs*, 101, 1–32 (1987).

[10]Lee Becker and Maxwell McCombs, The role of the press in determining voter reactions to presidential primaries, *Human Communication Research*, 4 (1978), 301–307.

+.70.[11] In local politics, voters' images of two candidates for mayor of Victoria, Texas, in the 1990s also significantly matched the descriptions in their local newspaper (+.60).[12] There are many other examples.

There also are examples of attribute agenda setting for public issues. The aspects of issues selected for attention by the media influence the public's perception of these issues. For a broad and recurring issue such as the economy, one set of attributes consists of the perceived causes and proposed solutions for the specific economic difficulties of the moment. Among the general public in Minneapolis, the correspondence between the *Minneapolis Tribune*'s agenda for these aspects of the economy and the public's picture of the economy was a strong +.81. Another set of attributes consists of the various arguments pro and con regarding the proposed solutions to these economic problems. In Minneapolis, the degree of correspondence there between the media and public agendas of attributes was less but still a substantial +.68. Discussion of the economy in the news had major influence on how the public were thinking about this issue.[13]

In a very different setting, a local environmental issue in the MidWest, there was a similarly strong level of correspondence (+.71) between the pictures in people's minds and local newspaper coverage on six aspects of a project to develop a large man-made lake in central Indiana.[14]

Which aspects of an issue are covered in the news—and the relative emphasis on these various aspects of an issue—makes a considerable difference in how people view that issue. From the pattern of the total news coverage, the public learns what journalists consider the important issues are and who the prominent public figures of the day are. From the details of this coverage— the agenda of attributes presented by the news media—the public forms its images and perspective about these issues and public figures.

Influencing the focus of public attention is a powerful role, but, arguably, influencing the agenda of attributes for an issue or political figure is the epitome of political power. Determining the way that an issue is framed—setting the ground rules for deliberation, if you will—can significantly influence the ultimate outcome. In the first year of George W. Bush's presidency, the specter of soaring electrical bills and sporadic power outages in California, coupled with rising gasoline and natural gas prices across the nation, easily propelled the energy issue onto the national agenda. But beyond

[11]David Weaver, Doris Graber, Maxwell McCombs and Chaim Eyal, "*Media agenda setting in a presidential election: Issues, images and interest.*" Westport, CT: Greenwood, 1981.

[12]Kenneth Bryan, Political communication and agenda setting in local races. Unpublished doctoral dissertation, University of Texas at Austin, 1997.

[13]Marc Benton and P. Jean Frazier, The agenda setting function of the mass media at three levels of information-holding, *Communication Research*, 3 (1976), 261–274.

[14]David Cohen, A report on a non-election agenda setting study. Paper presented to the Association for Education in Journalism. Ottawa, Ontario, Canada, 1975.

these dramatic effects on public attention, how was the energy issue to be framed? For the Bush administration, the priority framing was the need to produce more oil, natural gas and coal to meet the nation's energy needs. Framing the energy issue in terms of conservation was downplayed in Washington, D. C. but not by other voices across the country. How to frame this issue became something of an issue in its own right.

There are obvious implications here for the traditional journalistic norms of accuracy, balance and fairness. The traditional conflict narrative—the "he said, she said" school of journalism—juxtaposing the administration's position with the conservationist's position is grossly inadequate for reporting this situation. For a complex issue such as energy, there are many, many aspects to be considered, which is to say that there potentially is a vast agenda of attributes to be reported. The task for journalism is to go beyond stenographic coverage of the most vocal framers of an issue—even beyond in-depth investigation of their claims and assumptions.

True enterprise reporting means identifying as many of the aspects of an issue as possible and putting them on the agenda for consideration. But those are only the first steps in the natural history of an issue, the beginning of raising consciousness about it. The continuing news story is the lengthy process of public deliberation about this agenda, a process of working through that can eventually lead to thoughtful public policy decisions about the best course of action. This process of moving beyond initial public opinion to arriving at public judgment[15] is discussed in greater detail in Chapter 11. The initial point made here is that the news media have a central agenda-setting role in that process—identifying the major issues of the day and presenting the full agenda of attributes for those issues. There is nothing in this task that calls on journalists and the news media to abandon their neutrality or ideas about fairness and balance. It simply is a more systematic and responsible version of what the media presently do in a more willy-nilly way.

THE PUBLIC AND THE MEDIA

Although the influence of the media agenda can be substantial, information and cues about object and attribute salience provided by the news media are far from the only determinants of the public agenda. People still, at some point, decide for themselves what really matters to them; there is a difference between the importance attached to events by the media (and therefore initially by people) and the relevance of those events to people. The substantial influence of the news media has in no way overturned or nullified the basic assumption of democracy that the people at large have sufficient wisdom

---

[15]Daniel Yankelovich, "*Coming to public judgment.*" Syracuse, NY: Syracuse University Press, 1991.

to determine the course of their nation, their state, and their local communities. In particular, the people are quite able to determine the basic relevance —to themselves and to the larger public arena—of the topics and attributes advanced by the news media. The media set the agenda only when their news stories are perceived as relevant by citizens.

In many instances, the desire by journalists to tell a good story overrides thoughtful judgments about what the public really needs to know and blinds journalists to the public's depth of interest. The intensive news coverage on the Clinton–Lewinsky scandal spectacularly failed to set the public agenda and sway public opinion about President Clinton's ability and right to serve. Despite gargantuan play and persistent digging for the tiniest detail, "All Monica, all the time" wound up demonstrating only that the media voice has limitations. Overwhelmingly, the public rejected the relevance of that scandal as the basis of their opinion about the president's success or failure at governance. Surveys consistently showed that while people condemned Clinton the man, they continued to accept Clinton the president.

Clinton–Lewinsky was hardly the first time that journalists have misjudged the public's appetite and interest. Large portions of journalists' professional judgments about what should be on the news agenda are routinely ignored by the public, a pattern of behavior vividly reflected in the declining readership for daily newspapers. On a typical day in 1980, about two-thirds of the adult population read a daily newspaper. By the end of the century, this figure had slipped down to 57%. There is a similar decline in television news viewing, both for network television and local television.[16]

This decline in the size of the audiences of the news media as well as the presence—or, sometimes, absence—of specific agenda-setting effects by the news media can be explained by a basic psychological trait, the innate need within each individual to understand the environment around them. Whenever we as individuals find ourselves in a new situation, there is an uncomfortable psychological feeling until we explore and mentally grasp at least the outlines of that setting. Recall your first semester in college when, most likely, you were in a geographically and intellectually unfamiliar environment, or your initial feeling on moving to a new community or visiting a foreign city.

This innate need for orientation also exists in the civic arena. Voters in Austin, Texas, were asked to vote for or against the construction of a light-rail system by the local transit authority. In this situation, there was a very high need for orientation, at least among those citizens who intended to vote in the referendum. Few Austin residents really understood what light rail was or how the benefits and costs of light rail—which was to be paid for by an existing sales tax—compared to other options such as more expressways

[16]"*Facts about newspapers.*" Vienna, VA: Newspaper Association of America, 2000. For a comprehensive look at the news media, see Patterson, "*Doing well and doing good.*"

for automobiles. The Austin *American-Statesman* attempted to satisfy this need for orientation with extensive coverage and discussion on numerous aspects of the city's transportation problems.

Because it is a psychological trait, the degree of need for orientation varies greatly from one individual to another. For most individuals in Austin, there was a high need for orientation regarding light rail. They were concerned about the city's traffic problems but had little understanding of what light rail might contribute to the solution of this problem. For other individuals, there was little or no need for orientation at all. They just weren't interested and didn't intend to vote in the referendum.

Recurring situations in which need for orientation is typically high are party primary elections and local nonpartisan elections for judges, situations in which voters often have little or no information about the candidates. And every 4 years there is the high-water mark of national civic involvement and need for orientation as people briefly tune in to politics and make their decision about how to cast their vote for president. In all these situations, and many more, people experience a need for orientation, a need for some kind of mental map and understanding of where they are.

Need for orientation is defined by two components: relevance and uncertainty. Relevance is the initial defining condition that determines the level of need for orientation for each individual. If a topic is perceived as irrelevant—or very low in relevance—then the need for orientation is low. Individuals in this situation pay little or no attention to news media reports on this topic and, at most, demonstrate weak agenda-setting effects.

For individuals among whom the relevance of a topic is high, their degree of uncertainty about the topic determines the level of need for orientation. If this uncertainty is low, that is, they feel that they basically understand the topic, then the need for orientation is moderate. These individuals for whom a situation has high relevance and low uncertainty will monitor the media for new developments and perhaps occasionally dip into a bit of additional background information. But they are not likely to be avid consumers of news reports about the topic. Agenda-setting effects among this group are moderate.

Finally, among individuals for whom both the relevance and their uncertainty about a situation is high, need for orientation is high. These individuals typically are avid consumers of news reports about the topic, and strong agenda-setting effects typically are found among these individuals.

To demonstrate the usefulness of need for orientation in explaining the public's behavior, let's look at that high-water mark of American politics, the presidential election, and see how attention to the news media and their agenda-setting effects vary according to individuals' levels of need for orientation. Table 5.1 illustrates two distinct patterns: Both frequent use of the news media to follow the election and the agenda-setting effects of the news media on the perceived importance of the issues steadily increase with the

TABLE 5.1

Media use and agenda-setting effects by level of need for orientation

	Need for Orientation		
	Low	*Moderate*	*High*
Frequent users of newspapers, television and news magazines for political information	54%	63%	74%
Agenda-setting effect of television (issue agenda)	+.05	+.41	+.55
Agenda-setting effect of newspapers (issue agenda)	+.29	+.59	+.68

level of need for orientation among members of the public.[17] When the news media do provide information that citizens find relevant and useful in coming to a decision about how to cast their ballots, there is a substantial audience—and there is substantial media influence on the priorities that citizens assign to the issues of the day. In this situation, the public and the news media are partners in public life and a common search for understanding.

Suggestions for Additional Reading

Jay Rosen, *"What are journalists for?"* New Haven, CT: Yale University Press, 1999.
Maxwell McCombs and Amy Reynolds, News influence on our pictures of the world. In *Media Effects,* 2nd edition, Jennings Bryant and Dolf Zillmann, editors. Mahwah, NJ: Lawrence Erlbaum Associates, 2002.

---

[17]David Weaver, Political issues and voter need for orientation. In *"The emergence of American political issues,"* Donald Shaw and Maxwell McCombs, (Eds.). St. Paul, MN: West, 1977, pp. 107–119.

CHAPTER

6

Three Publics
for the News

The vast range of differences among individuals in their need for orientation about public affairs identifies three major publics for news: Information-seekers, monitors and onlookers. There is, of course, also a nonpublic, that 10 percent or so of the adult population who seldom follow news in any fashion: newspapers, television or online. Our focus here is on the three publics that are involved to varying degrees in public life and the use of news media.

Information seekers, who most closely resemble the idealized citizens of democratic theory, are persons to whom elections and a wide variety of public affairs are highly relevant. Typically, they make an effort to acquire a considerable quantity of information about public affairs because they have a high need for orientation. Some individuals are situation-specific information seekers because there is an immediate decision to be made—those high-need-for-orientation people in the election example presented in Chapter 5, Table 5.1 or many of the voters who went to the polls in Austin, Texas, to say "Yes" or "No" about light rail. Other information seekers have an abiding, long-term interest in some aspect of public affairs. In "*The American People and Foreign Policy*," Gabriel Almond called this group the "attentive public." These are persons with high interest in an issue, considerable knowledge about the issue, and a pattern of regular acquisition of new or additional information about the issue.[1] Similar attentive publics have been identified for a variety of other topics.[2]

---

[1]Gabriel Almond, "*The American people and foreign policy*." New York: Praeger, 1960.

[2]Jon D. Miller, "*The American people and science policy*." New York: Pergamon, 1983; Thomas Patterson, "*The mass media election: How Americans choose their president*." New York: Praeger, 1980; Serena Wade and Wilbur Schramm, The mass media as sources of public affairs, science and health knowledge, *Public Opinion Quarterly*, *33*(1969), 197–209.

There also is evidence of a general attentive public, that is, information seekers who routinely cast their net widely in the daily news report. Among the members of this public, there is a systematic and cumulative progression through three or four categories of information in the daily newspaper.[3] From the broad array of national and international news typically found on the front page and in the first section of the newspaper, this general attentive public moves on to reading local governmental news, then to other political news. If we define this general attentive public as those persons who regularly read all three of these types of news, it is about one in four or five members of the community. If we add reading the editorial and op-ed pages to our definition of the general attentive public—in other words, increase the requirement to regularly reading four types of news—then this public is about one in six or seven members of the community. Most individuals who immerse themselves this deeply in the daily newspaper also make extensive use of television news.[4]

Another public consists of monitors, those individuals who monitor or scan the ongoing stream of news for information specifically relevant to them and their lives. These individuals generally are satisfied with knowledge *of* the issues of the day rather than detailed knowledge *about* the issues of the day. Monitors become an attentive public only when an issue with rather immediate consequences for them moves onto the community or national agenda, something they see as a threat or an opportunity. As noted in Chapter 2, Schudson observed that this public based on a strategy of monitoring now has displaced the information-seeking public as the majority public.[5]

Although there is a long-running debate about whether the information-seeking public ever was the majority, there is considerable contemporary evidence that monitors, persons with only a moderate need for orientation about public affairs, now are the modal public. For example, there is the pattern of declining levels of newspaper reading and television news viewing already noted in this chapter. For newspapers, this decline is largely the result of frequent readers, those who regularly read a daily newspaper on four or five weekdays, becoming occasional readers, those who read a daily newspaper only a few times each week.[6] Large numbers of persons formerly with a high need for orientation now have only a moderate need for orientation.

When the entertainer Eddie Fisher, by divorcing Debbie Reynolds and marrying Elizabeth Taylor, revealed himself as someone likely to test the attentiveness of the public with a string of wives, *New York Times* columnist Russell Baker says he realized for

---

[3]Elsa Mohn and Maxwell McCombs, Who reads us and why, *The Masthead*, 32, 4 (1980–1981), 20–29.

[4]Leo Bogart, "*Press and public: Who reads what, when, where and why in American newspapers*," 2nd ed. Hillsdale, NJ: Lawrence Erlbaum Associates,, 1989, Chapter 7.

[5]Schudson, *The good citizen*, pp. 294–314.

[6]Bogart, *Press and public*, pp. 84–89.

the first time that "there might be a lot of things that were not worth keeping up with. This," he explains," "was a moment of liberation." ... Will ignorance of the exact cause of death, of the subcommittee's vote, or of the names of Eddie Fisher's wives come to be seen as a sign of a disciplined resistance to the blandishments of the current noise?[7]

Additional evidence that many persons are satisfied with no more than a moderate need for orientation is found in analyses of how people reach their voting decisions. A simple calculus based on a few orienting cues is sufficient for many: how a candidate stands on one or two issues that an individual finds particularly relevant or the images of the candidates based on a handful of attributes. "*Low-information rationality*, or 'gut' rationality, best describes the kind of practical reasoning about government and politics in which people actually engage," concluded Samuel Popkin in *"The Reasoning Voter."*[8]

A third public, onlookers, is those persons for whom civic life has little personal relevance. These are the individuals with a low need for orientation, persons for whom the daily newspaper and television news may be more of a pleasant distraction and source of entertainment than a source of orientation to civic life. Many of these persons are registered to vote, but they do not appear at the polls with any regularity. The fact that onlookers do make some use of the news media and do appear at the polls from time to time is cause for a degree of optimism. Onlookers are potentially reachable—and will become participants in public life—if the news agenda strikes a resonant chord.

Finding those resonant chords for all three of these publics means that journalists must be more than creators of interesting and compelling stories based on the traditional news values of journalism. Journalists must be communicators who are concerned about the effects—and especially, the lack of civic effects—of their messages on the public. More specifically, journalists and news organizations need to work at tailoring their messages to reach all three publics. One strategy used by many newspapers is to use summary boxes and graphics to highlight the key aspects of major news events, then present all the details in lengthy, more traditional stories. The boxes and graphics service the monitors and might even entice the onlookers. Detailed stories serve the information seekers. Online news sites can reach these disparate publics with attractive home pages and summaries complemented with hyperlinks that can take the audience deeper and deeper into the aspects of the topic about which they want more knowledge.

WATCHDOG ROLE OF JOURNALISM

The goals of the revered watchdog role of journalism typically include rooting out the malfeasance, conflicts of interest and corruption in public life.

---

[7]Stephens, *A history of news*, p. 291.

[8]Samuel Popkin, *"The reasoning voter: Communication and persuasion in presidential campaigns."* Chicago: University of Chicago Press, 1991, p. 212.

The news media are the public's surrogate looking over the shoulder of public officials, institutions and businesses. This tradition of investigative reporting is a steeple of excellence in the profession of journalism. But this watchdog role often is too confined to the actions of individuals in some narrow setting. Frequently, the focus is on indictable crimes. An expanded notion of this watchdog role will be more successful in gaining the attention of all three publics for the news.

When the city of Philadelphia built a new convention center, the city's news media were diligent in digging out instances of corruption in who benefitted from the disbursement of public funds.[9] But the larger watchdog role of questioning whether the city really needed this facility or whether these funds might be better invested in other public works was never on the media agenda.

In the summer of 2001, the Austin, Texas, *American-Statesman*— along with the city of Austin and the U.S. Attorney—was in diligent pursuit of what happened to the $1.45 million in public funding and another $3.70 million in private funding for Vision Village, a 4-year-old project that has yet to produce any of its promised 156 low-cost housing units. Pursuit of this story is an important watchdog function. But the larger watchdog role for all the local news media in Austin is the question of how to provide affordable housing for both the chronically depressed portions of the city and, increasingly, for middle-income citizens priced out of the market by the city's economic boom. It is likely that the Vision Village situation ultimately will be resolved by the civil and criminal courts. The judicial process will not resolve Austin's housing situation. But the Austin news media can put this situation on the public agenda and keep it there through the long period of working through to some resolution. It took Austin more than 15 years to settle the matter of building a new airport. Building individual housing is much more complex. In short, the watchdog role of the news media cannot be limited to an investigative series of reports—even if it wins a prize—or a running story on one aspect of a larger community situation.

The news media frequently are agenda setters. But what is the civic relevance and utility of the items placed on the agenda? Jay Rosen commented in *"What Are Journalists For?"* that "the point of having journalists around is not to produce attention, but to make our attention more productive."[10] News media need to be creative watchdogs and agenda setters scanning the horizon for the gaps in current public life. Part of this larger watchdog role is functioning as social radar, not just a chronicler of what government and other institutions are doing right now, whether good or bad. This means discovering the concerns of citizens and defining what the public needs to know in very expansive terms.

---

[9]Phyllis Kaniss, *"Making local news."* Chicago: University of Chicago Press, 1991.

[10]Jay Rosen, *"What are journalists for?,"* p. 295.

After extensive discussions involving a substantial cross section of community leaders as well as key members of the newspaper's own staff, the San Antonio, Texas, *Light* began 1992 with a full editorial page spread in the Sunday newspaper proposing that the community focus on eight specific issues affecting the city's children.[11] Although most newspapers try to stimulate public opinion with their editorial page, few systematically formulate such a highly focused editorial agenda and then follow through with extensive running news coverage. The effects were dramatic. Funding by the city of San Antonio for 10 children's programs increased by nearly $6 million that fall. The median increase in these programs was 13 percent, significantly exceeding the overall 9 percent growth in the city budget. Reflecting on this initiative's blend of the *Light*'s editorial voice with news coverage, the editorial page editor commented on the synergy between these two aspects of newspaper journalism and what is happening in the local community:

> If you have set the agenda well, have identified major needs in the community, then any conflict between the editorial and news roles of a newspaper will take care of itself.[12]

Looking toward the future economic well-being of their state, the Huntington, W. V., *Herald-Dispatch* and West Virginia Public Broadcasting (WVPB) jointly explored "West Virginia After Coal." Coverage of the issue included a statewide public opinion poll, a six-day newspaper series, and creation of a comprehensive database that documented how little of the $18 million in coal severance taxes distributed to the state's 55 counties and 234 municipalities supported efforts at economic diversification and worker training. Using new digital technology to create a three-hour, interactive "town meeting" from 10 different sites across West Virginia, "The Legacy Project" was broadcast on both the radio and television networks of WVPB during September 2000. These were the opening gambits of ongoing journalistic enterprise.[13]

THE ETHICS OF SETTING AN AGENDA

Daily and hourly decisions about the media agenda—what to include and how to play it, as well as what to omit—are among the most important ethical questions in journalism. Is the media agenda a valid effort to provide

---

[11] Marcus Brewer and Maxwell McCombs, Setting the community agenda, *Journalism & Mass Communication Quarterly*, 73 (1996), 7–16.

[12] Brewer and McCombs, Setting the community agenda, p. 14.

[13] *Civic catalyst*. Washington DC: Pew Center for Civic Journalism, Spring 2001, p. 10.

what the public really needs to know? One way of proving that the media agenda does provide what the public needs is to explicitly identify the civic utility of a news story.

An exercise that has proved useful in undergraduate journalism courses is one illustration of this idea of civic utility. For the first part of the exercise, the students cover three or four meetings of the city council and write their stories. Typically, these rather lengthy reports are a condensed "rearranged minutes" version in which the items on the agenda of the council meeting are reordered to reflect their news value rather than the chronological order in which they were taken up by the city council. For the second part of the exercise, the students select their best city council story—best in their own opinion, not necessarily the one that received the best grade. For each item covered in that story, written answers are required to each of these questions:

> Who in particular among the general public is the primary audience for this item?
>
> Why would they want to know / need to know about this?
>
> On the basis of the answers to the first two questions, does the story contain sufficient relevant information? Too much marginal or irrelevant information?

Finally, the students rewrite their story on the basis of their answers to these questions.

To put the matter in abstract terms, the students are asked to critique the civic utility of their reporting, and if they find it deficient, which they nearly always do, to produce an enhanced version. In some instances, the outcome of their critique is to shift substantially the prominence of an item on the media agenda. In other instances, the outcome is a change in the framing of the item or the addition of other aspects of the item to the news story. All these changes have important implications for what the public can do with information provided by the news media about their city council's actions.

This same kind of critique can be applied to other kinds of public affairs reporting and in an election year, particularly applied to how the interminable presidential campaign is covered. For decades, about one-third of the coverage has been devoted to the key issues of the campaign and the candidates' positions on these issues. This leaves about two-thirds of the coverage devoted to spot news about the campaign and its hoopla, to speculations about who is leading the horserace at that moment and is likely to win, and to analyses of campaign strategy and similar information that Joan Didion described as "insider baseball."[14]

During all these decades that issues have been relegated to a minority position in the news coverage, the issues also have been framed largely in neg-

---

[14]Joan Didion, Insider baseball, *New York Review of Books*, October 19, 1988, 19.

ative terms as polarized and frozen opinions on which there is little common ground and little possibility of finding any. Only rarely has this been a realistic account of the situation. In more recent decades, coverage of the candidates also has become increasingly negative. How much civic utility does all this information have? Vast amounts of money go into election-year coverage. What is the public dividend from that investment? Chapter 13 deals in detail with election coverage and how it can have more civic utility.

Of course, there are many other even more glaring examples in recent years of poor civic investments by the news media. A multitude of news organizations collectively spent tens of thousands of dollars camped out in front of Richard Jewell's apartment in Atlanta. It is doubtful that the public gained an iota of information that it needed to know from this harassment of a man falsely implicated in the 1996 terrorist bombing at the Atlanta Olympic Park. Other names that are familiar from their appearance in the center ring of a media circus are Elian Gonzalez, Monica Lewinsky, the Mendez brothers, O.J. Simpson, and U.S. Rep. Gary Condit. The list is long.

Journalism is a distinct form of mass communication precisely because it has a social responsibility for the nation's and the community's civic health. With the appearance of ever-larger media and communication companies, there has been considerable discussion about how the line between news and entertainment has become blurred and indistinct. Against this backdrop, Ed Fouhy warned one group of newspaper editors:

> If we do not change, we stand a very good chance of becoming increasingly irrelevant, except as another form of entertainment where there are already many more attractive forms of entertainment.[15]

The "change" that Fouhy had in mind was in enhancing the relevance of the news to the audience and public life. The declining audiences for news in all its forms—newspapers, national television and local television—underscores the need for change called for by Fouhy. But even among members of the news audience with considerable interest in the news, interest coupled with a strong belief in a civic duty to keep up with the news, there has been a dramatic decline in their attention to daily newspapers, network television news and local television news.[16] Access to the Internet and its myriad sources of news and information has stemmed, at best, a small proportion of this declining attention to news.

Audience members complain that much of the news has little relevance for them as individual members of the public, and critics complain that

---

[15]Quoted by Jay Rosen, What are journalists for?, p. 79.

[16]Paula Poindexter and Maxwell McCombs, Revisiting the civic duty to keep informed in the new media environment, *Journalism & Mass Community Quarterly*, 78 (2001), 113–126.

much of the news does little to facilitate the process of democratic government at either the local or national level. Public journalism with its call for
journalism to make public life go well has proved highly controversial. Why
the controversy? Isn't this call an explicit statement of journalism's long-
standing implicit beliefs about its responsibility to serve the needs of the
public?

CIVIC UTILITY OF THE NEWS

All three publics for the news intuitively grasp the idea of civic utility, and
among all three publics there are strong beliefs that much of what one finds
in the daily news lacks relevance. Public opinion polls and focus groups can
detail these views with considerable specificity—whether ascertaining
overall evaluations of news media performance or evaluations of the coverage about individual issues, public figures and other topics. This kind of research is needed on a continuing basis to measure exactly how effective the
news media are as public communicators, to measure how relevant citizens
find the content of the news media, and how much the public has learned
from this content.

Moreover, this research should go beyond general descriptions of how
the public responds to the daily news and measure the performance of the
news media against some very specific criteria. One source for these criteria
is the venerable Hutchins Commission report, "*A Free and Responsible
Press.*"[17] However, before reviewing the criteria for media performance advanced by that commission, some important aspects of its background need
to be noted. Although this report is most frequently discussed in the idealis-
tic context of social responsibility theory—one of the grand macrotheories,
along with the libertarian and authoritarian theories, of how the mass media
are organized in various societies[18]—the origins of this report were immi-
nently practical. The commission was suggested to University of Chicago
Chancellor Robert Hutchins by *Time* magazine founder and publisher
Henry Luce and substantially funded by Time Inc. However, the members
of the commission, distinguished academics and public officials of their
day, enjoyed complete freedom in their deliberations.

Their comprehensive analysis of the mass media, not just the news media
of their day but also movies and books, identified five requirements for a
free and responsible press in a democratic society:[19]

---

[17]The Commission on Freedom of the Press, "*A free and responsible press.*" Chicago:
University of Chicago Press, 1947.

[18]Fred Siebert, Theodore Peterson, and Wilbur Schramm, "*Four theories of the press.*"
Urbana: University of Illinois Press, 1956. Also see William Rivers and Wilbur Schramm,
"*Responsibility in mass communication,*" Rev. ed. New York: Harper & Row, 1969.

[19]"*A free and responsible press,*" Chapter 2.

- A truthful, comprehensive, and intelligent account of each day's events in a context that brings out their full meaning. There is already enough in this initial criterion of media performance to fill the questionnaire of a public opinion poll or discussion guide for focus groups. And numerous examples already have been offered here of gaps and irrelevancies in daily news coverage. But there is more to consider.
- A forum for the exchange of comment and criticism, a requirement that advocates of public journalism contend goes considerably beyond letters to the editor, op-ed pieces and occasional news reports on public hearings, civic debates and other incidental public affairs events.
- A representative picture of the various social groups that constitute American society, a requirement that has taken on considerable significance since September 11th. The importance of understanding people who trace their ethnic and cultural background to the Middle East, other parts of Asia, and to Latin America was further underscored by the 2000 Census with its detailed findings on the substantial immigrant population of the United States. It is also particularly important to take note of the long history of public reports seeking better understanding of racial relations and tensions in our country.
- Presentation and clarification of our country's goals and values, a requirement inextricably linked with the previous requirement because of the increasing cultural complexity of the country as a whole and its individual cities, towns and neighborhoods. Noting that the mass media are "an educational instrument, perhaps the most powerful there is," the Commission also observed, "The mass media, whether or not they wish to do so, blur or clarify these ideals as they report the failings and achievements of every day."[20]
- Facilitation of citizens' full access to information about the current state of public affairs. Facilitating full access does not ignore differences in an individual citizen's need for orientation or the existence of multiple publics for the day's news.

We do not assume that all citizens at all times will actually use all the material they receive. By necessity or choice large numbers of people voluntarily delegate analysis and decision to leaders who they trust. Such leadership in our society is freely chosen and constantly changing; it is informal, unofficial, and flexible. Any citizen may at any time assume the power of decision. In this way, the government is carried on by consent.[21]

To paraphrase a more recent *New York Times* advertising campaign touting that newspaper's extensive news coverage, "You may not read it all, but

---

[20]*A free and responsible press*, pp. 27–28.

[21]*A free and responsible press*, p. 28.

isn't it comforting to know that it is there." Especially in a time of declining political participation, maintaining the option for every citizen to participate in a knowledgeable way is critical.

There are three publics for the daily news, and news media have a responsibility to be effective communicators to all three. This requires careful professional reflection about the choices made each day for the media agenda. It also requires precise measurement of the public's response to this agenda, explicit feedback that measures the effectiveness of journalists as public communicators with a vital social role.

Suggestions for Additional Reading

The Commission on Freedom of the Press, "*A free and responsible press.*" Chicago: University of Chicago Press, 1947.

Robert D. Putnam, "*Bowling alone: The collapse and revival of American community.*" New York: Simon & Schuster, 2000.

CHAPTER
7

Technology and the New Millennium

People do not buy information technologies—they buy content, usefulness, and convenience at the point when they perceive value to match the cost.
—Roger Fidler, "*Mediamorphosis: Understanding New* Media"[1]

Much like those swelling waves that can move across the vast reaches of the Pacific Ocean, steadily growing in size and momentum until their gigantic flood engulfs some isolated island, a vast technological wave moved relentlessly across the 20th century and pounded onto our shores in this new millennium. Early in that century, radio—the first of the electronic mass media—supplemented the hundreds of newspapers and magazines. By midcentury, television added to the reach and power of mass communication, soon augmented by ever expanding cable television channels. As the century moved toward its close, the personal computer and the Internet opened a vast new universe of information, a combination of an international yellow pages targeted at specific individual needs and an international newsstand offering mass media from every corner of the world with every perspective on the day's news. Technological marvels—the gee-whiz stuff of feature stories—had created a gigantic wave of information.

Although there always has been a tendency to view new communication technologies as unmitigated blessings, as a panacea for our social problems, it also always has been the case that reality soon provides a corrective discount. This already is apparent in regard to the flood of information chan-

---

[1]Fidler, *Mediamorphosis*, p. 260.

nels now available to us. The lessons to be learned from Postman and Thoreau in this regard were cited at the very beginning of this book. More is not necessarily better.

MEDIA COMPETITION AND DIVERSITY

In elaborating why more is not automatically better, we preface our discussion of the situation here in the new millennium by reviewing a widely shared belief about mass communication, the belief that competition creates diversity. As the number of daily newspapers in the United States receded from 1,772 morning and evening papers in 1950 to 1,480 dailies at the end of the century, leaving more and more cities with a single newspaper voice and an ever-smaller number of companies owning a larger and larger proportion of the newspapers still publishing, critics viewed these trends with great alarm. In their view, the marketplace of ideas—the supply of news and opinion— became significantly less diverse when a competitor disappeared from the market and left a city with only a single daily newspaper.

In those earlier times when daily newspapers were the dominant mass media, the presence of competing daily newspapers in a community was taken as prima facie evidence of diversity in the supply of news and opinion. But was that true? Or, alternatively, is the menu of news and opinion available to the audience largely determined by the traditions and practices of journalists regardless of the ownership structure?

The traditions of journalism center on news values and ethical standards, such as balance and fairness, and the homogenizing influence of these traditions on news content have been traced as far back as the 19th century.[2] The routines of news gathering—for example, the organization of news beats, reliance on press releases, and covering events, many of which are staged specifically to attract press attention—further define the homogenous behavior of journalists across news organizations.[3] The social perspectives of journalism are a centripetal force for a centrist convergence on social and political issues.[4]

In short, this body of evidence on the sociology of news collectively predicts that news media competing in the same geographic and demographic markets will produce highly similar, not diverse, products. Back in the time

---

[2]Michael Schudson, "*Discovering the news: A social history of American newspapers.*" New York: Basic Books, 1978.

[3]See, for example, Leon Sigal, "*Reporters and officials: The organization and politics of newsmaking.*" Lexington, MA: D.C. Heath, 1973.

[4]Todd Gitlin, "*The whole world is watching: Mass media and the making and unmaking of the new left.*" Berkeley: University of California Press, 1980; Herbert Gans, "*Deciding what's news.*" New York: Pantheon, 1978.

outlets—and attempt to maintain some appearance of differentiation among them to attract an audience—is a major problem. Contemporary solutions to this problem have produced two trends: fragmentation and the blurring of the line between news and entertainment.

The news cycle—once a relatively clean dichotomy between morning and evening newspapers and a distinct set of television news programs spaced across the day—has grown ever shorter for all the electronic media. To reduce the sheer repetition of the same news over and over, new stories often are rushed onto the air or onto the web site in rudimentary outline on the flimsiest of sourcing. Audiences are bombarded with scattered fragments, many of which are later retracted. This approach to news reporting is more likely to produce bewildered citizens who are not sure how to assemble these scattered fragments into any meaningful mosaic.

But even this strategy is dependent on the existence of real news, which is a relatively scarce commodity. So the set of acceptable stories for the news report has expanded, a strategy that helps solve the problem of how to fill voracious newsholes and that offers the potential of creating synergy between the news report and other media products produced by the same corporation. In practice, the frequent result has been a blurring of the line between news and entertainment. The focus of the synergy often is a new television program or feature film that receives a level of attention far beyond anything that press agents or publicists of past decades would have imagined in their wildest fantasies. There is, of course, another form of entertainment that is wholly journalistic in its origin— scandals and sensational behavior. Once virtually the exclusive province of the supermarket tabloids, the last decade has seen a running catalog of these stories. O.J. Simpson and Monica Lewinsky were just the most visible tips of an ever growing iceberg. Journalists have always sought good stories to attract the interest of an audience. But in recent times this narrative imperative—the urge to tell a good story—has taken on startling dimensions. Is it possible that the deluge of these salacious tidbits from running stories that offer little more that the satisfaction of curiosity— some would say prurient interest—are linked to the steady decline in the news audiences for all media and in the continuing decline of public trust in the news media?[10]

---

[10]For detailed information on the decline in news audiences, see Patterson, "*Doing well and doing good.*" For a summary of the decline in public trust in the news media over the past 30 years, a review of the social science research on this trend, and an in-depth analysis of public trust in the media based on interviews with national samples of voters following the 1996 and 1998 national elections, see Stephen E. Bennet, Staci L. Rhine and Richard S. Flickinger, Assessing Americans' opinions about the news media's fairness in 1996 and 1998, *Political Communication*, 18 (2001), 163–182.

THE END OF MEDIA AGENDA SETTING?

A vast array of agendas are now readily available to the public, leading some social observers to predict the end of agenda setting as audiences fragment and virtually everyone has a unique media agenda that is a highly individualized composite constructed from a vast wealth of news and information sources. The result of these idiosyncratic personal agendas will be a public agenda characterized by diversity and the scattering of attention, some observers predict. Perhaps it is even incorrect to speak of a public agenda in these circumstances, they suggest.

This perspective on the future is the antithesis of the long-standing situation in mass communication characterized by large audiences receiving highly redundant agendas from the media. As previously noted, the initial observations in Chapel Hill, NC, of the agenda-setting influence of the news found substantial similarity—a median correlation of +.78—among the nine media agendas that were the dominant sources of news and information for voters. Obviously, this degree of similarity is not found across the total array of Web sites on the Internet, leading to the prediction that the era of agenda setting is coming to an end. But like so many prognostications about the magic of a new technology as the source of radical change, these predictions about the disappearance of any substantial agenda-setting influence simply may be wrong.

Predictions about the disappearance of agenda setting as a potent social force are grounded in a broad assumption that audiences will fragment and avail themselves of vastly different media agendas. Corollary to this assumption is the expectation that the redundancy across outlets characteristic of mass communication for many decades will be greatly reduced as niche media offer very different agendas. Moreover, there is the expectation that a substantial number of individuals will use a significant number of these multiple sources of news and information, patterns of behavior that will result in a large number of highly idiosyncratic personal agendas. At present, there is little evidence to sustain these assumptions.

Most of the news sites on the Internet are subsidiaries of traditional media, the online versions of newspapers, magazines and cable TV news channels. In this setting, it already has been noted that the popular buzzword synergy means amortizing the costs and increasing the profits of news by distributing the same basic content through numerous channels. It also is the case that, currently, the audiences for all Internet sites are very small. In short, the redundancy in the media agenda to which most of the public is exposed is likely to continue for at least the near future.

An additional major constraint on exposure to the agendas of multiple Web sites is time and effort. Few people have the time or wish to expend the effort to explore this virtual library in any depth except under extraordinary circumstances. Despite the plethora of sites that could be accessed, there already are suggestions of the existence of a news and information oligopoly in which a small number of sites command the largest proportion of the Internet users. Even when software allows members of the public to specify their categories of interest in advance, most people also want to know about the day's most important events regardless of the category in which they fall.

Under these circumstances, editors will continue to edit—that is select and summarize from the vast daily array of news. The fundamental nature of the front pages of newspapers and the opening segments of TV newscasts as a showcase for the day's most important events are likely to remain largely the same. There still will be a relatively homogenous media agenda, at least until someone invents a new kind of news that eclipses the traditional news audience. If that happens, it will be the result of journalistic creativity, not technology, and it will shift the agenda-setting influence of the news media to a new source.

New technologies offer vast new opportunities. But technology is only a means of distribution, not a substitution for content that citizens find compelling in their personal and civic lives. Success in the new millennium will be measured by the quality of journalists' daily response to the question, "Why do we do journalism?"

Suggestions for Additional Reading

Roger Fidler, *"Mediamorphosis: Understanding new media."* Thousand Oaks, CA: Pine Forge Press, 1997.
Neil Postman, *"Amusing ourselves to death."* New York: Penguin Books, 1985.

Part II

Part II

CHAPTER

8

The What

Journalism recovers itself when it ceases to be a device for dealing with the problems of journalists and becomes a method, cultivated by journalists, for dealing with the problems of men.
                    —Paraphrase of John Dewey's famous quote about philosophers[1]

For 60 years, the prevailing model of public affairs journalism in the United States has been one in which reporters and editors "cover" people and events that they deem to be important or newsworthy. They write about those people and events with the aim of informing citizens about public matters. The flow is from source through journalist to citizen.

Reporters and editors assume the posture of neutral observers, detached conveyors of information. Sometimes because of the complexity of events, they become analysts and interpreters, but only out of the necessity of helping people understand, not out of any admitted desire to affect the flow of events. The goal is to present information in a "journalistically objective" way—that is, fairly, honestly and accurately, with proper balance—and let citizens make of it what they will, do with it what they will, or ignore it altogether.

Limiting the role to neutral observer and conduit is both compelling and convenient. It allows journalists to focus on the singular task of transmitting information and absolves them of any other responsibility. The simple, straight-line model is based on several assumptions:

- That citizens are, or at least should be, intensely interested in being well-informed about public affairs and thus are eager receptors of what journalists consider important.

[1] Cited in Louis Menand, "*The metaphysical club*." New York: Farrar Straus Giroux, 2001, p. 362.

- That "truth" put to the test in fair contest will always prevail over "untruth."
- That new information has intrinsic, utilitarian value simply because it is new.
- That governments and other institutions are inevitably the "actors" and citizens the "acted on" and therefore the journalistic conduit need only be one-way in design.
- That "giving people what they need" and "giving people what they want" are distinct functions, and the former is far more important and valuable than the latter, which is somehow seen as fundamentally threatening to journalism's foundations.
- That the public sphere, the private sphere and the journalistic sphere are necessarily separate, like atoms held in eternal stasis by immutable natural forces and connected only by the flow of information.

These assumptions, each of which is arguable in today's world, form the basis for journalistic reliance on the model of detached observer and transmitter of information from source to citizen. As we saw in Part I of this book, that efficient though simplistic model has ceased to well serve either public life or journalism, and a more sophisticated model is needed.

The new model challenges the dynamics of the old one and involves two fundamental shifts: repositioning journalists and repositioning citizens, that is, challenging the stastis model of the three spheres. "Positioning" in this usage is not a mechanical event; it is a conceptual one. It is the picture in the journalist's mind of the relationship among citizens, journalism and public life; conceiving of those spheres not as in stastis but as a dynamic.

Nothing in this model suggests that journalists abandon what is commonly called journalistic objectivity, that is to say, the imperative to be fair, honest, accurate, and clear-eyed about facts. It does suggest that journalists move away from the idea of detachment, that is, the mistaken notion that journalists are and necessarily must be separate from the consequences of their decisions.

While the terms *objectivity* and *detachment* are often used interchangeably and sometimes in the same sentence, as in "detachment and objectivity are fundamental to good journalism," our model makes a distinction between the two. That distinction is best illustrated this way. Jonas Salk discovered a vaccine for polio. As a professional scientist, he had to be objective about the facts of his research, if for no other reason than that scientific protocols require that other scientists be able to replicate his results. But he was not detached. He did not enter the lab willy-nilly, wondering what he might find. He had a purpose: finding a cure for a dread disease. And he cared very much whether or not he discovered it.

Another way of thinking about the difference between objectivity and detachment is this. You want your doctor or lawyer to be objective. That is, you want her or him to be clear-eyed and clear-minded about the facts of your case, to be truthful with you about it, to be fair in the way your case is treated. But you do not want him to be detached. You want her to care very much about a successful resolution of your situation.

Likewise with professional journalists, it is both possible and desirable to be objective without being detached. Objectivity reflects intellectual and professional honesty; detachment reflects a lack of concern.

Moving away from DE-tachment does not mean moving to full AT-tachment; for instance, caring about whether a problem is solved does not mean dictating how it is resolved. Detachment–attachment do not lie on separate sides of a single, fine, bright line; they constitute a continuum. Imagine two vertical lines, one to the left of this page, the other to the right. The one on the left represents the pole of total detachment that positions journalists at a far remove from the events they cover, free from all conse-quences of their decisions, able to say, "We just tell the news and have no re-sponsibility for anything other than doing that fully and honestly." The other line represents total attachment, which positions journalists as fully en-gaged in the events they cover. Just as full engagement by journalists is ob-viously unacceptable, so is the other position. Journalists in today's world necessarily must operate somewhere in that middle ground between the poles, for reasons that have to do with the preservation of both the profes-sion and democracy.

The paraphrase from John Dewey at the opening of this chapter reflects a concern about the usefulness of the profession of journalism. Dewey's orig-inal comment was about his profession, philosophy. As a pragmatist, Dewey was interested in having the work of philosophy resonate in society in a useful and important way. It cannot be influential if the central concern of philosophers is insular—the problems of philosophy. What is necessary is to address, among other things, the concerns of democracy and its people, Dewey felt.

Traditional journalism can sometimes slip into insularity, in part because journalists fail to distinguish between objectivity and detachment. Defining and operating within that middle ground between dangerous total detach-ment and equally dangerous total attachment is what the balance of this book is about.

Sampling the News

All the reporters in the world working all the hours of the day could not witness all the happenings in the world.

—Walter Lippmann, *"Public Opinion"*[1]

Only a limited number of journalists are available to monitor daily life. Even if there were an infinite supply of journalists, the capacity of the various news media could not accommodate all their reports. This is true even though with Web sites and all the other new technologies, there is far more capacity than at any time in the past. Even this enlarged capacity poses a problem for the public, whose available time, range of interests, and span of attention are limited. Of necessity, the reported and received news is a tiny sample of all the daily happenings in the world.

More important, the news is a highly idiosyncratic sample of each day's events and situations. A grab bag of professional routines and traditions largely inherited from the past define how journalists sample the world around them—what they pay close attention to and what they ignore as they prepare their news report for the public. More than 75 years ago, Walter Lippmann talked about the beat system and its dominant underlying rationale that news is not a mirror of social conditions but the report of an aspect that has obtruded itself.[2] Good sources for information about situations in which daily life departs from its normal, mundane channels include the police station, fire department and court house. The contemporary expression, "If it bleeds it leads," is a culmination of this perspective about news that results in

---

[1]Lippmann, *"Public opinion,"* p. 338.

[2]Lippmann, *"Public opinion,"* p. 341.

some local television news relying on a heavy diet of stories about accidents, crimes and fires. In less spectacular fashion, the beat system expanded to include a wide variety of officials at all levels of government—everything from the local zoning board to the White House—is a productive source of reports and statistics about nonroutine events that are grist for the journalistic mill. Of course, not everything that occurs at these locations or that is reported by these routine sources of news is sampled by journalists, only those occurrences that pass muster in terms of the traditional litany of news values.

The resulting sample of the day's happenings that is presented to the public is a highly peculiar one, a set of events mostly involving government officials in some role and heavily weighted toward conflict and bad news. Nowhere is this latter aspect of the sample—conflict and bad news—more obvious than in the reporting of presidential campaigns over recent decades. Think about the total set of events that make up a presidential campaign each day or each week. Then compare the sample presented in the news. To use the language of mathematics and polling, it is not a representative sample.[3]

In public opinion polls, which have become a staple of both the news media and political campaigns, achieving a representative sample of the public is the central goal. The core idea is to convey an accurate picture of the prevailing views among the public. To achieve this representative sample of the public, pollsters utilize the technique of random sampling, a procedure in which at the outset of the selection of persons to be interviewed for the poll, every person in the relevant population has an equal opportunity to be selected.

Obviously, this kind of random sampling would not work for observing the occurrences of each day. The vast majority of these occurrences are of no interest to the general public. Who cares that Fred had a beer after work and talked sports with his friend, Bob; that 86 people renewed their drivers' licenses that day in Austin, Texas; or that Amtrak Train 27 arrived in Chicago five minutes ahead of schedule? Actually, there are a few people who care about each of these things, but these people are not a very large proportion of the public. So, to use the technical language of sampling, journalists employ the technique of stratified sampling. That is, they divide the events of the day up into various categories or strata. To use Lippmann's term, a simple, first cut at sampling the day's events is to group them into two strata, the obtrusive and the unobtrusive. The latter strata, the unobtrusive and routine, are deleted from any further consideration, just as many political pollsters define persons not registered to vote out of their picture of political trends. One of the purposes of stratification is to focus attention on particular kinds of events or persons.

A major part of the problem with existing definitions of news, which fewer and fewer members of the public find relevant, is that the strata of daily occurrences defined as newsworthy are too narrowly focused. Put the

---

[3]A detailed example is in the Prologue of Patterson, *"Out of order."*

other way, too many strata are defined out of the picture. First, consider the sampling of obtrusive events from a limited set of news beats. This yields a considerable amount of news. But many times the public—and investigative journalists—are interested in an overall situation, not just the obtrusive events that are the latest aspect of the larger situation. The news about the rapid growth of Austin, Texas, is more than the latest zoning controversy or the month-long detours on the interstate highway. These are small bits in the larger mosaic of urban growth. On a broader scale, the information collected in the national census every 10 years provides a wealth of news stories that detail not just how many of us there are in the United States, in each state, and in each community, but what kinds of people live in what kinds of homes and how all this differs from 10 years earlier. This is one example of news stories about who we are and how we live our lives. There are many others that present the full picture, not just the obtrusive events. Our stratified samples of life in the world around us need to encompass general situations as well as obtrusive events.

These stratified samples of events and situations also need to extend beyond the traditional journalistic strata of government, sports, finance and entertainment. Even in the unfamiliar language of sampling theory, the names of these strata sound familiar because these are the typical sections and topics of most daily newspapers. Those are the strata routinely sampled each day by journalists. But there are many other strata that could be sampled to provide the public with news that it finds newsworthy and relevant.[4]

Until very recently, religion was one of those strata defined out of the news picture. Some years ago, a public opinion survey asked Maryland residents in the area adjacent to Washington, D.C., who were the important community leaders in their area. This roster of leaders was compared with the sources quoted in the Maryland section of the *Washington Post*. You can guess the results. Clergy were high on the public's list of leaders, but seldom quoted in the newspaper. There were numerous other disparities. Many strata of activities that are relevant and interesting to the public are ignored by most news organizations.

STRATIFIED SAMPLES OF REALITY

Because the tradition of news beats and news values is so familiar and so entrenched in the thinking of journalists and because the concept of stratified

---

[4]For a comprehensive analysis of news sources used by various forms of broadcast journalism, see Stephen Reese, August Grant and Lucig Danielian, The structure of news sources on television: A network analysis of 'CBS News,' 'Nightline,' 'McNeil/Lehrer,' and 'This Week With David Brinkley,' *Journal of Communication*, 44 (Spring 1994), 84–107. Even within a stratum of news, the range of sources is often constricted. See the extensive discussion on indexing theory and traditional journalistic norms in the October–December 1996 issue (13, Number 4) of *Political Communication*.

sampling is so unfamiliar, we review the basic outlines of the idea of stratified sampling before discussing some creative ways to apply this idea to
gathering the news. Pollsters divide people into groups—in other words,
they stratify society into two or more groups—for two basic reasons.

One of the reasons already mentioned is that it makes no sense to interview
certain kinds of people. In an election poll, only the opinions of persons eligi-
ble to vote are meaningful. In a survey of what people watch on cable TV or
how people use the Internet, only the responses of those who actually sub-
scribe to cable or who have access to a computer and use the Internet are
meaningful. Stratification is used on many occasions to exclude some people
and narrow the focus to others whose behavior is more relevant.

At other times, the reason for stratification is to emphasize the focus on
certain kinds of people, usually people characterized by some relatively rare
trait or pattern of behavior. If you want an accurate assessment of the political views of American Indians in North Carolina or of persons who contribute money to political candidates, a stratified sample is needed to find
enough of these people who are relatively rare in the population in order to
make any accurate assessment of their views or behavior. In sum, we as
journalists stratify to sharpen our focus, sometimes to exclude those in
whom we are not interested so we can attend to the others, sometimes to ensure that we have an accurate picture of an important group.

Sampling people, even in strata that are defined by some very rare trait, is
much simpler than that the task that faces journalists; sampling all the happenings in the world. There are a lot of people in the world, even in the
United States or even in a single community. But it is a finite number. In contrast, the number of happenings in the world each day, even the number of
happenings in a single community in a single day, is essentially infinite.
There are many, many ways to define and describe the happenings of the
day. Identifying the relevant ones—defining and sampling the key strata of
happenings—is the creative aspect of journalism.

Of course, journalists have been constructing stratified samples that included some of the happenings of the day for decades. News beats and the
various sections of the newspaper are one way of stratifying the happenings
of the day. Each is an outcropping of some aspect of life in the nation or
community. But the traditional set of news beats and newspaper sections
aren't the only—or even the best—way to find news that is meaningful to
the public, even with some of the new wrinkles added in recent years such as
religion, shopping malls and high-tech.

In the face of yawning disinterest among large segments of the public, especially among young adults, journalists need to understand two fundamental points. First, any plan of news coverage is, in the abstract and of
necessity, a stratified sample of the day's happenings. Most aspects of reality are ignored; a few are heavily sampled. Second, there are many ways to

construct a stratified sample of reality, many interesting and useful ways to define the newsworthy strata of your community. Creative journalists will identify these strata in innovative ways to produce stories that an audience will consider as important news, something that involves more of their life than just passing the time.

There are no fixed or magic answers to the question of how to sample the day's happenings. But there are some very familiar starting points for thinking creatively about how to sample the important realities of everyday life and how to develop new kinds of content and insight to the public.

Probably near you at this moment is a highly detailed catalog of the activities in your city that occupy a substantial part of everyone's time every day—the yellow pages. All those classifications tell you how most people spend most of their week, either as the providers of those different kinds of goods and services or as the consumers of them.

To sharpen the focus on what is important to people in your city, compare the yellow pages in your town with those of other cities and towns. Social scientists have done that as a way of profiling the differences among communities. You also can compare the current yellow pages with editions from previous years to track key changes in the community.

In Austin, Texas, the yellow pages reveal that there is not a major bank in town today with the same name as any bank doing business here a decade ago. What are the implications of this upheaval in the financial community? At the same time, the continuing growth of the metropolitan area is indexed by a significant increase in the number of retail outlets listed for the two major grocery chains and two major drugstores, a quick indicator of how much growth there has been and in which parts of town the growth has occurred. For another slice of daily life in Austin (pun intended), the four largest pizza companies now have more than 60 locations spread across the metropolitan area. Even a yellow pages-based stratified sample can provide insight into a community's dynamics and suggest trends that can be pursued with more detailed reporting.

OTHER GUIDES TO IMPORTANT ACTIVITIES

There are many other readily available guides to the activities that engage major segments of people's lives every day and thus provide clues about their interests. These range from time-use studies on how people carve up each 24 hours into a variety of activities to the economic analyses of each state's gross domestic product, the total dollar value of the goods and services produced. Of course, at the individual level there also are numerous analyses of how consumers spend their money. In the hands of creative journalists, these statistics become the indicators and the foundation for news stories that address key aspects of daily life, news stories that will resonate with readers and viewers because they describe and explain important parts of people's lives.

Another key indicator of events and situations that resonate with the public because they impact daily life are occupational surveys, both those indicating major shifts and those indicating stagnation. A computer company that didn't exist 20 years ago now employs 21,000 people in central Texas. Investigating and explaining the implications of that for life in that metropolitan area—daily life for everyone, not just those 21,000—can keep a newsroom full of journalists busy for years. At the other end of the spectrum, there also are major implications for daily life in communities where the mix of occupations shows little change over time. This situation often indicates current or impending economic and civic stagnation. And, of course, in both changing and unchanging situations, there is likely to be major news about the dominant occupational groups in the community, whether they are government workers, low-level service providers or high-profile professionals. What people do for a living tells you a lot about a community and can be important clues to news about the activities that engage people every day.

In a similar fashion, the way that land is used—and how that may have changed over the past decade—also tells a lot about a community and points the way to news that resonates with the public. Nearly half of the land in downtown Los Angeles is dedicated to automobiles in the form of streets and parking facilities and about half of the land in downtown Syracuse, N. Y., is tax exempt because it is the site of various governmental and religious facilities. These facts are the opening gambit to major analyses about life in these cities. Every county has extensive property tax records, most urban areas have detailed zoning maps, and many areas have extensive urban development plans. These lead to news stories ranging from the fifth generation family farm about to become part of the new expressway to how much money people pay—and are likely to pay in the future—in property taxes.

CURIOSITY AND UNDERSTANDING

If telephone books, compilations of economic statistics, and zoning maps seem mundane, it is because they are. These are the detailed maps of everyday life in the community, the state, and the nation, much of which is mundane and ordinary. But there are leads to many fascinating individual stories in these sources, and in the aggregate they trace the trends that impact people's lives in very significant ways every day. These trends are the stuff of compelling news stories that resonate with readers and viewers and engage their close attention.

To characterize these sources and many similar ones as unproductive lodes of journalistic ore is to commit two fallacies. The first fallacy, which already has been discussed, is to miss the opportunity to broaden the sampling of events and situations in the local community and to retreat into narrow, shopworn definitions of news that engage fewer and fewer members of the public each year. The second fallacy is to miss the critical distinction between curiosity and understanding. Both are innate, embedded psychological characteristics. Most people are curious, and most people seek to understand significant segments of the world around them.

Last year, the short three-block-long street that loops into our immediate neighborhood from the main thoroughfare suddenly filled with fire trucks and police cars, lights flashing and sirens blaring. About as many neighbors turned out on the street that evening as turn out for the annual neighborhood picnic. People were very curious about what emergency might account for the sudden appearance of all these vehicles. The explanation—a high intensity lamp had overturned and set a rug on fire in the living room of a neighbor's home—satisfied their curiosity. The crowd quickly melted away, and the incident was largely forgotten.

Do a simple experiment. Park a police car, or some other emergency vehicle with flashing lights on top, in front of some commercial establishment. A crowd is likely to quickly gather. People are curious. There are many journalistic examples, of course, and the most famous of recent times may be the O.J. Simpson "chase" in Los Angeles in which TV news helicopters followed O.J. and his friend for miles as they drove along the freeways. In subsequent weeks, both television and newspapers continued to feed this curiosity with dozens and dozens of news reports. People are curious and these kinds of news reports do draw an audience. But in the long run, do people really care? People slow down to stare at automobile accidents along the highway. They are curious, but this is not an endorsement for more automobile accidents or more coverage of fender benders. People are curious about many things, but most of these are not things that they really desire to understand. Why? Because these things have little or no bearing on their personal lives.

For a brief time, people were curious about Monica Lewinsky. Her misadventures had all the elements of superlative gossip. But most people quickly grasped the essentials, including the fact that this sex scandal had little or nothing to do with President Clinton's governance of our nation. The press' persistent salacious framing of the scandal guaranteed both its short-term appeal to curiosity and the lack of any long-term link with the need to understand the political environment.

Many topics can briefly arouse people's curiosity, but individuals are highly selective about the topics that they seek to understand. This desire to understand significant aspects of the surrounding environment is innate within humans—and is quite distinct from mere curiosity. Chapter 5 detailed the need for orientation inherent in our psychological makeup that explains why there are newspaper readers and TV news viewers. But unless the content of the news media satisfies this basic need for orientation, these audiences will continue to shrink. The news media are frequently described as people's windows on the world. But to what extent does the view through this window provide personally relevant surveillance of the world around us? This is a key ethical question and organizing principle for journalists' techniques of sampling the news.

Beyond this question about the topics that the news media offer for public attention and scrutiny, there is the critical follow-up question of how well the public understands these topics. Recall that attention and comprehension are the two aspects of the communication process involved in the agenda-setting role of the news media. In this chapter, we have talked about focusing journalists' attention on topics that the public finds relevant. Extending this discussion to comprehension, in Chapter 10, we talk about framing news stories in ways that engage and inform citizens. Subsequent chapters place this discussion of news stories that gain public attention and understanding in the larger context of public judgment and deliberation on the critical topics of the day.

Suggestions for Additional Reading

Walter Lippmann, "*Public opinion.*" New York: Macmillan, 1922.
Bartholomew Sparrow, "*Uncertain guardians: The news media as a political institution.*" Baltimore: Johns Hopkins University Press, 1999.

CHAPTER
10

Framing Stories and Positioning Citizens

You know how to write a news story: Gather the facts, ask and answer the question "what's this story about?" and start writing. It becomes a reflex, the habituated use of "who, what, when, where, why and how" to tell a story. The story is about the set of facts at hand or the event just witnessed. And if your objective as a journalist is only to relay that information, the task is relatively simple: organize the facts or events in terms of their importance within the overall narrative and pound away. You still have some decisions to make, of course, but they are constricted by the chosen objective, which is to relay information.

As we have seen, however, in a world flooded with the commodity of information packaged as news, the value of a few hundred more words added routinely to that flood is marginal and likely to be lost on inundated, if not inured, audiences. That 21st-century reality was succinctly captured by David Shenk in *"Data Smog"* when he wrote, "New information for its own sake is no longer a goal worthy of our best reporters, our best analysts, our best minds. Journalists will need to take a more holistic approach to information as a natural resource that has to be *managed* more than *acquired*."[1] Illustrating the point, Shenk quoted a former editor of *Editorial Research Reports*, Marcus Rosenbaum, this way: "If you do a NEXIS search on welfare reform, you're going to have 53,000 hits. What do you do with that? But if I can give it to you in 8,000 words, that will be interesting."[2]

---

[1]Shenk, *"Data smog,"* p. 170.
[2]Quoted in Shenk, *"Data smog,"* p. 170.

Managing the flood of information to give it coherence and relevance offers a very different challenge to journalists than does merely relaying new information. It requires additional steps and skills. The issue, when we move beyond merely relaying facts in some routinized order, becomes one of framing.

A journalist can no more produce an effective story without a basic framing strategy than an artist can paint a picture without one. The artist isn't going to show us the entire world in a picture, only parts of it. So she must make decisions about which parts to show and how to arrange them within the dimensions of the chosen canvas to accomplish her purpose. The decisions are about content, for sure, but they are also about perspective and point of view. And, just as important, they are decisions about the viewer.

When our artist sets out to produce a painting, she makes certain initial assumptions about the viewer: where the viewer will be standing in relation to the picture (usually straight ahead but not always, such as in the case of a large mural or a ceiling painting), what light will play on the picture and in what way, and what the overall viewing environment will be. Therefore, when artists start a work, they must first mentally position the viewer within the viewing environment, and that positioning directly affects the content and other details of the work. That's true with the simplest painting, and it is also true of the simplest news story. The journalist, in addition to making decisions about content, also, usually unconsciously, positions the reader.

Here's an example of how framing and positioning choices affect content and approach. We as journalists want to write a story about an aspect of campaign finance reform. The new elements we have are these:

- A new report shows that a U.S. senator must raise thousands of dollars every day, week after week, to pay for a re-election campaign.
- We have come across an interesting and ironic phenomenon. Freshman House members can't get lobbyists on the telephone, a reversal of the historic order of things. A major lobbyist and campaign contributor tells us that he dodges such calls because "I know they're just after money," and others corroborate that.
- A substantial portion of the campaign funds will be used to purchase 15- and 30-second television ads because the candidate who spends the most money on television almost always wins.
- We have the latest report on the huge amounts of money that political action committees and other lobbying groups give to incumbents. We have good anecdotes about the tawdry wheeling and dealing that occurs: the fund-raisers and the direct solicitations and trade-offs.

We believe that people need to know these facts, so we set out to tell them. But using the same set of facts, we can frame that story in different ways, and different frames position the reader-citizen differently.

A. W can approach the story in a way that positions the reader as a passive spectator, which is the way most such stories are framed: "Look at what those people in Washington have to do to raise money. Isn't it a circus?" is the thrust of this framing.
B. We can frame the story to position the reader as a victim: "Look at what those people in Washington are doing to you, and there's nothing you can do about it!"
C. Or we can construct the story to position the reader-citizen as a stakeholder and potential participant: "They're raising millions of dollars to influence your vote with 15- and 30-second commercials, and it works because you allow it to work" is the thrust of this framing.

The first two frames begin and end with a narrow concept of the political process—it is something happening out of the reach of the reader-citizen who should perhaps be bemused by it (the spectator framing) or offended by it (the victim framing). In neither case do we assume that the reader-citizen has a role to play. The third framing positions the reader-citizen as a part of the problem, a stakeholder and a potential actor. In other words, it defines the situation as a public problem involving everyone, not simply one of the shenanigans in far-off Washington, D. C. involving only the direct players.

The effect of framing is often subtle, but it is real and therefore it needs to become a conscious act, not a reflexive or accidental one. Facts do not frame themselves; reporters frame facts. People reading each of the three stories would have a very different perception both of the situation and how it affects her: In story A, something to be commented on and perhaps disgusted about; in story B, something somehow damaging to the reader, but far beyond reach; or, in the case of story C, something to think about and potentially act on; a situation in which reader-citizens understand their stake in it and could play a role, no matter how small.

None of these framings is unreasonable. Each story can be accurate. Each can be balanced, fair, reliable and interesting. In short, each story can meet the traditional journalistic tests. The way the story is framed depends totally on the reporter's mind-set and purpose, which means that the reporter should make a conscious choice among alternative framings based on a fully developed idea of who is being addressed and for what purpose.

If we as reporters hold in our minds a Walter Lippmann-esque picture of citizens—remote, unengaged and unengagable, mostly incapable and uncaring—we would probably settle for one of the first two frames. The same would be true if we had no thought-out vision. The framing would be one most interesting or exciting to us, probably one of the first two: positioning the reader as a spectator or a victim.

If our vision as reporters, however, is more in line with John Dewey's, we would want the readers to understand their stake in the situation, how it fits into their world, and what they might do about it, and we would frame the story with that purpose. Keep framing is mind as you as citizens watch newscasts and read newspaper stories. Ask the question, How does this story position the citizen—as victim, or spectator, or member of an audience to be entertained, or as a stakeholder and potential actor? What would have been needed to frame it differently: more facts or simply a different approach? What might have been accomplished, in addition to telling the news, if the framing had been different?

A word needs to be said here about purposefulness in the context of story framing. If our answer as reporters to the question, "What's this story about?" is a narrow one—that the story is about the set of facts as we have them in hand—the answer is sufficient only for the purpose of arranging those facts in some sort of journalistic order. The facts become a narrow, episodic story that we write, some people read and react to, and we all move on to the next set of facts or transient situation. We have told citizen-readers once more that they are merely spectators or victims and not a part of a public empowered to act.

If, however, our answer as reporters is that the story is about a public matter that can yield to public response, then we have a broader purpose: giving people a road map for change, if they perceive that change is necessary. But even if most people perceive that change isn't needed or wise or possible, the properly framed story is yet enriching beyond that initial purpose. Framed in the most useful way—positioning the citizen as a potential participant—the story and others framed in similar ways begin to describe a world that is not far removed from average citizens, a world in which they are involved and for which they share responsibility, no matter how small. As Jay Rosen suggested, they begin to describe "a useable present."[3] Consistently framing stories in that inclusive way begins to alter the alienating picture that traditional, reflexive journalistic techniques have projected. The habit of traditional, exclusive framing helps account for the helplessness that many citizens feel about the political process and other aspects of public life. The different framing, the inclusive one, would move beyond only describing what is wrong to also imagining what going right would look like.

As noted at the opening of this chapter, journalists have habituated the traditional framing of news stories. It's a practice based on the "five W's and an H"—who, what, when, where, why and how. Effective public affairs reporting that seeks to help people engage in public life needs to take that formula deeper, to ask a more complex yet clarifying set of questions.

Some newspapers that have adopted the broader purpose of helping people engage as well as giving them news make use of a variation of the "five W's and an H" that was originally developed at the *Virginian-Pilot* in Norfolk, Va. These thoughts are not only applicable to reporting and writing but also have value as a way to think about other editing decisions, such as when (and even if) to start a project or story, when is a story actually ready to print, when does it really need to go, and what are we as reporters trying to accomplish by reporting the story?

---

[3] Jay Rosen, The master of its own domain.

Who
... cares about the issue?
... is affected?
... is responsible (not just to blame)?
... needs to be at the table (but perhaps is not)?
... ought to be talking about it?
... has concerns about it?
... has tackled this before?

What
... is the array of choices available and what are the potential conse-
    quences?
... does it mean to the citizen?
... would the proposal do or is it designed to accomplish?
... are the values behind it; and are they in conflict or in common?
... things do people need to know to form an intelligent judgment?
... don't we know?
... remains to be done?
... would success look like?

When
... do people need to have the information?
... were things different, or did it begin?
... will it become obvious?
... should dialogue lead to action?

Where
... is this headed?
... are the impacts going to be, beyond the obvious?
... are the best entry points for citizens?
... is the common ground (are most people on this)?
... should the conversation(s) take place?

Why
... do we care about this?
... are we writing this now (is it the most useful time)?
... is this happening?
... is this happening now?
... does the community need this discussion?

How
... does it affect public life?
... did we get here?
... does it encourage deliberation?
... will this help the public decide?
... long should the conversation take?

FRAMING CONFLICT

If everyone agreed about everything, democracy would look quite different. It would have no need of courts and legislatures or leaders and followers. But in any society in which people have free choice, they will inevitably disagree about those choices simply because people are individuals with different needs and ideas and values. Over centuries, humans developed such institutions as courts and legislatures as a way of mediating their inevitable conflicts civilly and safely. Individuals who are able to rally large numbers of people around specific ideas become leaders, at least for those ideas.

The differences in ideas and values inherent in democracy means that public affairs reporting is often about conflict—between individuals, among groups, between institutions and people, and between institutions. After all, the key question of democracy is, "What shall we do?" and the structure of our democratic institutions provides a way of answering that question.

Unfortunately, coverage of public affairs often loses sight of the fact that conflict is only one step in a larger process of searching for resolution, that is, finding an answer to "What shall we do?" Too often in public affairs reporting conflict in and of itself becomes the central narrative and the larger context is ignored. This occurs for a number of understandable reasons:

- Conflict is inherently interesting. Since people first began to talk to one another, it has been central to story-telling because it is central to life. Tales of the clash of people with the elements of nature, the struggle for food, the battles over territory and possessions were both interesting and useful when passed from person to person.
- Conflict is exciting for the journalists who deal with it.
- Conflict is an accessible, alluring and pliant narrative device for writers.

But relentlessly searching for and exploiting conflict to the exclusion of the totality of the process of public affairs is both disingenuous and dangerous. In his landmark book, "*Why Americans Hate Politics*," E.J. Dionne Jr. zeroed in on the problem of false and artificial conflict in our public affairs. Writing in the context of the two dominant ideologies in American politics, he argued:

> Liberalism and conservatism are framing political issues as a series of false choices. Wracked by contradiction and responsive mainly to the needs of their various constituencies, liberalism and conservatism prevent the nation from settling the questions that most trouble it. On issue after issue, there is consensus on where the country should move or at least on what we should be arguing about; liberalism and conservatism make it impossible for that consensus to express itself ....We are suffering from a false polarization of our politics, in which liberals and conservatives keep arguing about the same things when the country wants to move on.[4]

---

[4] E. J. Dionne Jr., "*Why Americans hate politics*." New York: Touchstone, Simon & Schuster, 1992, p. 11.

Because polarization of issues is useful and attractive to ideologues, including politicians, Dionne said, most Americans, who are not at either extreme on most issues, are, or feel they are, left out of the discussion. Their "leaders" are not talking about the same issues that most concern most Americans and are not talking about them in the way that most Americans would. Therefore, inevitably, Americans feel alienated from public affairs, grow cynical about them, and turn to other matters, leaving the field to the ideologues and extremists.

For journalists, Dionne's analysis should be cautionary because journalists must face this hard question: Where do these Americans who hate politics learn most of what they know about politics?

From journalists, that's where.

When public affairs journalism merely reflects the content of the politicians' discussions, it unavoidably conspires in the maintenance of those false choices and helps ensure that the consensus that might exist will not be expressed.

Journalists have at least two major incentives to do more than merely reflect continuing false ideological arguments. The incentives are obvious and practical:

- If people are not engaged in public affairs, they have no need of the journalists who write about public affairs.
- Journalism (as an expression of free speech) and democracy are fully interdependent; one cannot exist without the other. Journalism can be no stronger or resilient than the democracy that supports it; democracy can be no stronger or resilient than the journalism that supports it.

Journalists also have a subtler, but equally important, obligation to do more than simply reflect the ongoing false choices. If the re-engagement of citizens so critical to an improved democracy is going to occur in today's information-rich but increasingly information-complicated world, the journalism it is dependent on must work toward that re-engagement.

The objective is not to try to make politics-hating Americans love politics; the objective is to do journalism in ways that allow citizens to see the possibilities that engagement presents. This cannot be accomplished by merely reflecting the political environment constructed by political leaders and their handlers. Something else is required, and story framing is the primary tool for providing that something else, particularly the framing of stories that arise, as many do, out of inherent conflict.

Two emotional and seemingly intractable issues provide examples of different ways of framing conflict: gun control and abortion. In both cases, most reliable surveys show that a consensus of sorts already exists: a substantial majority of Americans believe in some firearms limitations, at least on handguns and automatic weapons, and a substantial majority of Americans believe abortion should be allowed under at least some narrow circumstances. In both cases, only about 15 percent of Americans are at each end of the continuum that ranges from "never" to "always" on abortion and gun control. Yet the discussion of those issues—and the coverage of those discussions—are usually framed at the extremes.

- For example, a typical story about the annual *Roe vs. Wade* anniversary demonstrations in Washington, D.C., and around the nation begins with, "The two sides of the abortion issue clashed on the streets near the Capitol Thursday." While it is true that those demonstrations involve people representing the two extremes of the issue ("never" and "always"), it is inaccurate to suggest that there are only two sides to so complex an issue. In fact, it is well-established that a great majority of Americans feel some ambivalence on the issue; they are somewhere between the two extremes. But when the activities—and the coverage of the activities—frame the issue only at the extremes, at least two unfortunate things happen: 1) the issue is rendered as one incapable of solution because the extremes are so far apart and the vast middle ground is invisible and 2) most citizens do not see themselves as part of the discussion, so they turn away from it.
- For example, Charlton Heston, president of the National Rifle Association, which is at the "never" end of the gun control spectrum, is shown at the 2000 NRA convention theatrically holding up an old musket and intoning in his best "Voice of God" manner, "They'll have to pry it from my cold, dead hand." No one except a tiny majority of people at the other extreme of the gun-control spectrum has suggested any law that would deprive him of that old musket or any weapon remotely like it. Yet the coverage in all news media seized on that conflict-ridden moment and thereby once again framed the gun-control argument as both intractable, because of the gulf between the extremes, and as not including most citizens because, again, a great majority of people say they favor some reasonable limits on some types of weapons.

Not many issues carry the emotional load of abortion and gun control, but many issues remain in uneasy and shifting status for decades as the extremes struggle for a bit more leverage here or there. Reaching final settlement on such issues is unlikely because of the strong emotions and core beliefs involved. As a result, Dionne's analysis is again validated. Liberals and conservatives keep arguing about the same things while the country wants to move on.

Failure to find resolution on such emotion-laden issues need not stand in the way of the public moving on to more pressing and resolvable issues. But they do stand in the way in large part because the style and extent of the coverage of them. Coverage that consistently frames those core issues only at the extremes helps those issues to become controlling: to become litmus-test issues by which people and actions are judged, and thereby become huge hurdles to progress on any issue.

Journalistic decision makers, from reporters to top editors, could help the nation move on to more pressing and more resolvable issues by a more accurate, thoughtful and purposeful framing. When the two extremes of the abortion issue march on Washington, D.C., both the individual stories and the total coverage—including emphasis and placement—should reflect the true status of the polarized minority extremes and put them in proper context. When Charlton Heston talks about "my cold dead hand," the reporting should carefully point out that only the most extreme gun-control proponents would suggest trying to pry that old musket away from him.

Allowing, in either case, the extremes to frame the issue unchallenged perpetuates not only the great divide between the extremists themselves but also discourages the majority of people in the middle from trying to engage the issue or join the discussion. Such framing results in a reinforcement of the feeling that public affairs are something dominated by extremists and ideologues who operate far beyond the reach of average people. It positions the reader-citizen as outsider, victim, spectator rather than potential participant.

STAKEHOLDERS AND THEIR STAKES

The purpose of framing conflict differently, that is more inclusively, is to help citizens understand their role as stakeholders in the issues of democracy, in answering the question, "What shall we do?" The possibility for the resolution of an issue is remote until several things occur, including the public's consciousness being raised about the importance of an issue, the public's stake in it, and the possibilities of resolution.

Most traditional reporting of public affairs, however, merely raises consciousness without considering the possibilities of resolution, and too often raises consciousness in a way that fails to point out the stakes that citizens and groups of citizens have in the issue and how those sometimes-conflicting stakes work for and against each other.

Deciding what to do is a matter of balancing choices and consequences. This balancing best occurs in a public framework rather than a private one. In other words, citizens facing the choices need to operate in a larger context than their own personal stake, although finally, that's where most choices wind up being made.

Journalists can greatly facilitate this process by framing the "choice work" broadly. One of the first, and still most notable, examples of a newspaper framing a critical issue this way was the 1996 coverage by *The Colorado Springs Gazette* of a local school bond issue. Colorado Springs, Colo., site of the Air Force Academy, is a complex community. It is home to a large contingent of retired military people who tend to conservatism but also contains a vibrant and more liberal element of younger people with children. Its climate and proximity to the Rocky Mountain resort areas attract its share of environmentalists and other causists of all stripes. The city's voters, three-fourths of whom did not have children in school, had not passed a school bond issue in recent history, and the school system had many needs.

Stephen A. Smith, the *Gazette*'s editor at the time, decided to use the occasion for an experiment. He and his staffers identified four distinct groups who had a stake in the bond election: taxpayers with children in school, taxpayers without children in school, school personnel such as teachers, and students. Two reporters were assigned the task of writing about the issue from the point of view of members in each stakeholder group. Although using those groups as a starting point was not in itself unusual, what distinguished this effort was the way the stories were reported and presented.

A traditional approach would have been to interview members of each group and juxtapose their views, using the conflict inherent in the situation to do "on the one hand, on the other hand" stories. Such framing positions the reader-citizen as a spectator at a debate or a juror in the jury box, requiring the reader to sort through the issue based on directly contending arguments. Such stories can have high emotional content, but they also can leave the reader merely confused about or disgusted with the whole situation.

The Gazette approach was quite different. The reporters interviewed more than 30 people from each group with the idea of coming to truly understand— and perhaps even appreciate—the differing positions. They then produced four different stories, each one designed to synthesize those views, that is, to make the arguments for that group's point of view. Because the reporters were assuming the responsibility of distilling many views into a reasonable-length story, they rigorously checked back with their sources after the stories were written to insure that their representations were accurate.

The newspaper printed those stories on separate days, each carrying a label making clear that the story was from that group's point of view. That step of presenting each story in isolation from the others was a crucial one for two reasons:

- It gave each group's view a "clean shot," presenting it without the contravening static that would have been present in on the one hand, on the other hand presentation.
- Just as important, it gave readers, including members of each stakeholder group, the opportunity to read and consider each group's views in a calm, relatively unconflicted atmosphere.

In effect, the newspaper's approach cooled the atmosphere a bit and allowed for true deliberation. It positioned the reader-citizens as people facing a complex and serious issue in which they and other people had an important stake rather than positioning them as people listening to an argument.

The newspaper did not fail to cover the usual heated rhetoric of various sides but played those stories under the dominating umbrella of the stakeholder series rather than allowing those conflict-ridden stories to be the main feature. It had not been the newspaper's aim to help pass the bond issue, though that is in fact what happened. Rather, its objective had to been to help the community have a civil conversation about its choices rather than allow the usual contending sides to frame the issues in a vacuum. It was in that sense that the experiment was a success.

The newspaper staffers, particularly the reporters and editors directly involved in the stakeholder exercise, learned a great deal not only about the issue and the people in the community but also about their potential roles as journalists. The community itself learned, for it witnessed and participated in a deliberative exercise aimed at answering the core question, "What shall we do?" Such events build civic capital, that is, a body of experience on which the community can draw as other choices present themselves.

Suggestions for Additional Reading

Cheryl Gibbs and Tom Warhover, *"Getting the whole story."* New York: Guilford Press, 2002.

E. J. Dionne Jr., *"Why Americans hate politics."* New York: Touchstone—Simon & Schuster, 1992.

Positioning Ourselves as Journalists

The purpose of democracy is to answer the question, "What shall we do?" In a representative democracy such as that in the United States, an important subsidiary question is "Who should decide what we shall do?"

As we saw in Chapter 3 (this volume), thoughtful people can disagree about the role the average citizen can or should play in answering those core questions. Walter Lippmann insisted that the average citizen was capable of playing only an oversight role: voting representatives in or out on the basis of self-interest and the level of personal comfort he or she felt. John Dewey argued that the average citizen could be and needed to be much more directly engaged in instructing those representatives. Michael Schudson and Robert Putnam extended the discussion in relation to today's society.

One need not decide whose ideas are closer to reality to think about possible roles for citizens and journalists in public life. Where should journalists imagine themselves positioned in the democratic equation?

The traditional position, that of the detached observer, reflects Lippmann's views that democracy functions best when left to experts and elites; the modern world is far too complex for average citizens who are not capable of absorbing and putting to effective use the information that floods in on them. Therefore, the reporter's role is to expedite the conversation among decision makers and support the exchange of information about events. Newspapers, the medium that dominated news gathering when Lippmann was expressing his philosophy, need relate to average citizens only on matters of procedure such as voting, and, as noted earlier, Lippmann's minimal expectation was that citizens would vote for the "ins" if they felt things were going pretty well and for the "outs" if they felt things were not going well.

Lippmann's philosophy, then, positions journalists as potentially among the elites and apart from citizens. It requires little of journalists in relation to average citizens except to act as an effective conduit to citizens on the limited occasions when that seems necessary and appropriate. This positioning immediately causes problems, as is readily seen in the disconnect between journalists and average citizens. Detached, elite observers quickly lose touch with the people they seek to serve and are seen by those people as part of "them" instead of "us." As a result, journalists have little regard for the citizens or confidence in their abilities, and citizens, in turn, view journalists with suspicion and invest little credibility in what they say.

Other positionings are possible, desirable and more useful to the ends of democracy. If journalists believe that citizens are capable of active participation in governing themselves beyond casting an occasional vote, then they must adopt a position that allows the voices of citizens to come through to them and through them into their work. Jay Rosen expressed this as "starting where citizens start."

The traditional view of the journalist as conduit between decision makers and from them to citizens is immediately changed when journalists start where citizens start. Now the journalist has additional conductive roles: from citizens to decision makers and from citizens to citizens.

This positioning makes a broader democracy more likely but does not entirely solve the problem. As we saw in Chapter 5 (this volume) on agenda setting, it is not possible for journalists to act merely as conduits, for there is far too much information to pass along. Therefore, journalists necessarily become selective in what they pass along, and it is in the act of selecting that the journalist's values and worldview are unavoidably applied.

So positioning oneself as a journalist in a democracy that works requires an additional calculation: deciding what values or beliefs one will bring to the task of filtering information. We suggest four.

1) Democracy works best when people are broadly engaged in it.
2) Average citizens, given information and a way to discuss its implications, are in fact capable of reaching sound public judgment.
3) Representative government does not mean that citizens surrender their authority to those they elect; they place them in office as instruments of the public's will. The fact that elected representatives can nevertheless, at least between elections, override the will of the public is an important safeguard against the potential tyranny of the majority.
4) Democracy works best as a conversation in which people discover what they have in common—problems, opportunities, and concerns—and take the responsibility for responding to those problems, opportunities and concerns.

Given those beliefs, how do journalists position themselves to incorporate those problems, opportunities and concerns into their work and thus play a role in the equation beyond simply telling news, yet not compromise such important considerations as fairness, balance and appropriate journalistic objectivity?

Three tools can help:

- Understanding how public judgment comes about.
- Developing new listening skills and techniques.
- Recognizing and valuing deliberation.

Each tool plays a part in connecting journalists with citizens, thus helping bridge the gap that developed under the traditional model of public affairs reporting that left citizens out of the equation and contributed much to their existing alienation from both public life and journalism.

We deal first, and in some detail, with Daniel Yankelovich's important research on the issue of public judgment because it undergirds the others.

"COMING TO PUBLIC JUDGMENT"

That is the title of a seminal book in which Yankelovich explained the phenomenon of public judgment and how it is formed.[1] His book suggests ways in which the hand of citizens can be strengthened to return balance to the democratic equation, how the quality of public conversation can be improved, and how public officials and journalists can listen to what citizens have to say.

Whether the issue is large or small, the democratic way of dealing with problems is to strive for a resolution that everyone can live with, that benefits more people than it harms, and that recognizes and allows for differing opinions and values but nevertheless helps settle the issue so that the public's business can move on.

Public judgment, Yankelovich explained, is far more complex than mere opinion. In his three decades of research into public opinion preceding publication of the book, he developed ways to distinguish between off-the-cuff public opinion reflected in most statistical surveys and true public judgment.

A public judgment is "the state of highly developed public opinion that exists once people have engaged an issue, considered it from all sides, understood the choices it leads to, and accepted the full consequences of the choices they make."[2]

Reaching public judgment about important and complex issues can take years, and implementation of the judgment can take just as long as reaching it. For instance, the United States reached public judgment about women's rights decades ago after more than a century of debate, but aligning that determination with life's realities is still a work in progress.

---

[1] Yankelovich, "*Coming to public judgment.*"

[2] Yankelovich, "*Coming to public judgment,*" p. 6.

Sometimes public judgment is reached, but moving on to other matters is thwarted because of the determination of people who strongly disagree with the judgment. Such is the case with abortion. For years, every reliable survey has shown that 12 percent to 15 percent of the people are opposed to abortion under any circumstances; 12 percent to 15 percent favor abortion at will; 70 percent to 75 percent fall somewhere between those extremes and would allow it under some circumstances, which is the situation reflected in existing law. The surveys seem to indicate a strong majority have settled in the middle—a substantial public judgment has been reached—yet the loud struggle goes on in legislatures and the Congress every year, the initiative being taken and the issue framed by the groups at the margins as they attempt to alter existing law and practice. The lesson of the never-ending abortion debate may be that when opinions are based on core values, even a substantial public judgment cannot be permanently implemented.

The public reached judgment very quickly in 1999 in the matter of President Bill Clinton's liaison with a White House intern, deciding that although his actions were to be condemned, they did not want him removed from office because of them. That consensus only grew broader and deeper during the months of investigations and the eventual impeachment proceedings.

This is not to argue for or against any of those judgments but rather to demonstrate that public judgment arrives in many ways and at differing paces, and the effects of it differ greatly.

Yankelovich's definition of public judgment distinguishes between simple opinion based solely on instinct or information and judgment based on deliberation, which is "the thoughtful side of the public's outlook, the side that belongs with the world of values, ethics, politics and life philosophies rather than with the world of information and technical expertise."[3]

"In our era of proliferating public opinion polls and endless lamentations about how poorly informed public opinion is, an astonishing amount of confusion exists about the relationship of information to judgment," he wrote.[4] The confusion exists, he said, because experts and journalists assume that judgment must be based on quality information; that only an "informed" citizenry should be attended to and is capable of making "right" judgments about issues.

In fact, Yankelovich contended, public judgment finally is based less on information than on values. He quoted Everett Ladd of the Roper Center for Public Opinion Research, who wrote:

> Opinion research in the U.S. does reveal a public strikingly inattentive to the details of even the most consequential and controversial policies. ... But the research also indi-

---

[3]Yankelovich, "*Coming to public judgment,*" p. 7.

[4]Yankelovich, "*Coming to public judgment,*" p. 7.

cates great stability and coherence in the public's underlying attitudes and values. Americans show themselves perfectly capable of making the distinctions needed to determine what Harwood Childs called "the basic ends of public policy" and of pursuing those logically and clearly.[5]

In other words, public judgment contains a strong values component that need not be based on accurate or detailed information to express the public's point of view and underlies its recommendations to its elected representatives.

Thus, journalists and experts who decry the public's lack of information and therefore discount its judgment are missing the point and adding to the perilous gap between them and citizens.

In his book *"The Magic of Dialogue,"* Yankelovich said this about the process of public judgment:

> My research shows that the public's judgments are rarely the result of careful analysis of factual information. The public reaches its judgments through a different process than experts claim for themselves. Experts assert that their views are grounded on information, experience and analysis. The public must be doing something different. The public is generally poorly informed, doesn't do much analysis, and on most policy issues has little direct experience.
>
> The public, I have learned over the years, forms its judgments mainly through interactions with other people, through dialogue and discussion. People weigh what they hear from others against their own convictions. They compare notes with one another, they assess the views of others in terms of what makes sense to them, and, above all, they consult their feelings and their values. The public doesn't distinguish sharply between facts and values, as journalists and social scientists do. Indeed, dialogue draws heavily on feelings and values. Of course, information is important. But information stripped of feelings is not the royal road to public judgment; dialogue, rich in feelings and values, is.
>
> Here we have one of the keys to why public judgment may be sound and mature, even wise, though ill-informed. I have long suspected that something is seriously amiss in our conventional paradigm of knowledge, with its razor-sharp distinctions between "objective" facts and "subjective" values. In reaching its judgments through dialogue, the public is harking back to pre-scientific ways of knowing. These may actually have greater validity for the important questions of living together than current theories of knowledge.[6]

This idea, of course, is unsettling to journalists who, as Yankelovich and others, including Michael Schudson, have pointed out, operate on the model of the informed citizen as the key to successful democracy and who build their approach to their jobs on that model.

---

[5]Yankelovich, *"Coming to public judgment,"* p. 20. The Ladd quote is from Everett Carl Ladd, *"The American polity: The people and their government."* New York: Norton, 1985, pp. 315–316.

[6]Daniel Yankelovich, *"The magic of dialogue."* New York: Simon & Schuster, 1999, pp. 25–26.

True public judgment, once arrived at, reflects values rather than information because of the complex way in which the public arrives at the judgment, Yankelovich contended. The process involves three stages: consciousness raising, working through and resolution. He described them this way:

- Consciousness raising is "the stage in which the public learns about an issue and becomes aware of its existence and meaning. ...When one's consciousness is raised, not only does awareness grow but so does concern and readiness for action."[7] In other words, people decide: We have to do something about this. But what? And how?
- Working through can be complex and time-consuming, for it involves individuals having second thoughts—that is "resolving the conflict between impulse and prudence"[8] accepting new (and sometimes unsettling) realities, and resolving conflicts among the competing values that they hold. In other words, working through involves cognitive, emotional and moral calculations.
- Resolution occurs only after successful consciousness raising and working through, and the accumulated mass of that effort then reflects a public judgment.

Yankelovich pointed out that too often journalists and experts assume that consciousness raising—which journalists are expert at and dearly love —leads directly to public judgment. This miscalculation occurs because of the journalists' and experts' elevation of information over values. People, with or without much information, refer to their core values and beliefs in forming their opinions. When consciousness is raised by new information that challenges those values and beliefs the working through phase is essential before resolution can occur.

The heart of Yankelovich's analysis is that leaders can help the working through process—and thus expedite the arrival at public judgment—once they recognize the necessity of it. Yankelovich formulated "Ten Rules for Resolution" as a guide in helping the public come to judgment on issues.[9] Although the rules were not written specifically for journalists, they are useful for journalists as a way of understanding what's needed for public judgment to occur.

His rules are adapted here for journalists. Note that many of them require journalists to have an idea of what the public thinks and feels. Thus, it is clearly necessary for journalists to hone their skills at public listening.

---

[7]Yankelovich, *"Coming to public judgment,"* p. 6.

[8]Yankelovich, *"Coming to public judgment,"* p. 135.

[9]Yankelovich, *"Coming to public judgment,"* pp. 160–176.

Rule 1: To Bridge the Gap Between the Public and Experts, Learn What the Public's Starting Point is and How to Address It

Application.   Experts—and journalists—almost always start at a different place from citizens: health care costs, for instance. Knowledgeable people know it to be a problem of technology and aging population. Many citizens see it as an insurance problem: If I and everyone else have adequate health insurance, there won't be a problem. Journalists need to understand—through research and other means such as careful listening—where the public is and begin at that point.

Rule 2: Do Not Depend on Experts to Present Issues

Application.   Jargon is the defensive wall against invasion of the elite inner circle by outsiders. And even if that were not the case, some common words have different subtle meanings for experts than for the general public. For instance, arms control means balance of power to experts but means arms reduction to most of the public. In an increasingly complex world, the public must depend on experts for information, but information isn't the same as wisdom. Experts often come fully equipped with bias and their own solutions, either intellectual or emotional, and often when they present issues, they frame them wrapped in preconceived solutions.

Rule 3: Learn What the Public's Pet Preoccupations Are and Address Them Before Discussing Other Facets of the Issue

Application.   Whether broadly held ideas are rational or irrational, serious or trivial, there's no way to advance a discussion until those pet ideas and theories are addressed. Sometimes merely recognizing their existence is enough to get things moving. Often if we as journalists know what those pet preoccupations are, we can marshal the facts to address them. For instance, most people think the problems of poverty and welfare could be greatly eased if "people would go to work." No useful discussion can be had until the facts of that are presented and understood. But journalists have to learn first what those preoccupations are and avoid making assumptions about them.

Rule 4: Give the Public the Incentive of Knowing That Someone is Listening ... and Cares

Application.   For newspapers, this can mean hosting in our pages an active exchange of the views of ordinary people; writing about situations in which people accomplish things because their voices are heard by institutions; and fostering exchanges between ordinary people and institutions.

Rule 5: Limit the Number of Issues
at Any One Time to Two or Three at the Most

Application. This is simply a matter of capacity. Resist the urge to run from one consciousness raising to another.

Rule 6: Working Through an Issue is Best Accomplished
When People Have Choices to Consider

Application. Most people get information about issues already packaged in a view or with a preferred solution, or they quickly adopt their own. Getting alternatives onto the table is crucial—and it often must be done by us as journalists. Choices have consequences, and it's up to us to explain those. Some choices are mutually exclusive, and it's up to us to explain those clearly: You can't cut taxes but keep services, for instance.

Rule 7: Take the Initiative in Highlighting the Value
Components of Choices

Application. Here's where journalists have the biggest challenge in engaging people. Remember the values component of working through—it's absolutely fundamental to the way people come to judgment. People's opinions and judgment are always based on some sort of balancing of values, conscious or unconscious. But most people cling to their values and don't give much credit to the different (read "lesser") values of others.

First, distinguish between technical components and value components of the choices. We as journalists have lots of technical experts who can express alternatives, all of which may work to solve the technical challenge. But first, we need to resolve the values. Values identify the desired results; technical considerations are used to reach them. Unfortunately, technical experts often come with values biases that they (or we) may or may not be aware of.

For instance, what sort of prison people build—we have the technical ability to build any sort we want—depends on whether people believe that prisons are for rehabilitation or for punishment, or what proportion of each they consider most important. That values issue must be resolved before the technical solutions are applied. But the public almost always skips the values part.

Rule 8: Help the Public Move Past the "Say Yes to Everything" Form of Procrastination

Application.   Confront people with the consequences of their opinions. They can't cut taxes and not cut services. They can't pass mandatory sentencing laws and not build new prisons and add court capacity. Choices have consequences and journalists must relentlessly confront people with them.

Rule 9: When Two Conflicting Values are Both Important, Highlight the Possibilities for Tinkering to Preserve Some Elements of Each

Application.   This is pretty self-evident and the heart of democratic compromise. But getting people who feel strongly one way or the other to move can be very difficult. People must understand that they need not surrender their core beliefs to make progress on an issue. Abortion, for most people, is a classic example.

Rule 10: Be Patient

Application.   Pacing is everything. As journalists, we might have to go over the same ground several times, returning to the issue again and again. This is not a component of traditional journalistic operation. We are constantly moving on to the next new thing, whether or not the old thing has been either well-understood or resolved. Reaching public judgment can take years on some issues, but we'll get there more quickly if we work out and follow a deliberate process for getting there.

Yankelovich's rules as adapted for journalists clearly begin to answer the question of how journalists position themselves to incorporate in their work the four values mentioned earlier and play a role in the democratic equation beyond simply telling news. By understanding how public judgment comes into being and incorporating the ideas into their reporting and writing, journalists can avoid several traps:

- Expecting that raised consciousness is sufficient to create solutions.
- Ignoring the core role that values play in public life.
- Failing to incorporate into reporting the array of choices that are available.

- Portraying tough issues as a hopeless clash of conflicting values when, in fact, possibilities exist for common ground.
- Resisting the temptation to flit, honeybee-like, from one news "flower" to the next.

EFFECTIVE LISTENING

At the heart of the disconnect between journalists and citizens is a learned disregard on the part of journalists for the opinions and desires of ordinary people. Much of our routine experience as journalists feeds that disregard. After all, traditional journalistic practice deals primarily with the people and institutions that need to be covered, that is, watched and written about: public officials, institutional leaders and experts in various fields. Little time is left to hear from ordinary people whose views and desires at any rate are often wildly out of touch with "factual reality" as journalists understand it. Journalists interpret this as an information gap caused by ordinary people's ignorance or lack of interest when in fact the gap can also be the result of differing values, differing rates of information absorption and varying levels of interest.

When traditional journalism wants to get the views of the people, it almost always seeks them en masse, with surveys, or anecdotally, with random interviews. In both cases, the brief questions asked are answered off the top of the head, and the responses usually reflect underinformed, knee-jerk opinion. Certainly they do not reflect judgments based in deliberation.

Journalistic judgment about the value of ordinary citizens' opinions is also influenced by repeated tests of the public's level of information recall: Name your city council member. Who is the chief justice? Who was the second U.S. president? The results are almost always distressing and lead to the conclusion that ordinary people are hopelessly ignorant and certainly unworthy of much attention, if not downright dangerous.

Such experiences, however, can be misleading because those traditional reporting devices are shortcuts designed to turn around stories or get quotes in a hurry; that is, they reflect something *journalists* are trying to demonstrate rather than a true exploration of what's in peoples' minds and hearts. Discovering that requires conversation, including different ways of listening.

When journalistic interest in public opinion stops at that level, a great deal is missed that can inform journalistic practice. Not recognizing and doing something about that disconnect leads to errors in story framing, news judgment and overall focus that can make the journalistic product seem, to ordinary people, wildly out of touch with *their* factual reality. People interpret this as a credibility gap caused by what they see as journalists' elitism or lack of interest in the real world as citizens see it.

One way to begin to repair the mutual disconnect and play a more useful role in the democratic equation is to become better listeners and to cultivate the habits of what can be called public listening. The pressures of daily journalism, the 24-hour nature of news and most journalists' instincts invite, perhaps demand, a particular way of listening to the world: Our ears are open for stories, for good quotes, for conflict, for the unusual. This necessarily means that the usual, the routine, the mundane interests and concerns of most people are neither sought nor heard and being unheard, do not become part of the calculation when decisions about news and story content and framing are made. The result is a fatal disconnect; a mutual dissonance that makes the journalistic product less useful than it could be. Cultivating the habits of public listening requires deliberate effort, either organized or informal, either as a staff or as individuals.

ONE FORMAL PROCESS

Beginning in 1995, The Pew Center for Civic Journalism and The Harwood Group experimented with methods of public listening involving the staff of *The Wichita Eagle*. The result was a model that offers both a way of organized listening and a way to know more about how issues move within a given community. The results were published in a booklet called *Tapping Civic Life: How To Report First, and Best, What's Happening In Your Community.*[10]

Out of the experiment, Richard C. Harwood and his staff developed two key concepts: layers of civic life and types of community leaders.

The researchers identified five layers of civic life where very different kinds of civic conversation occur: official, quasi-official, third places, incidental and private. Each has its own unique qualities and each offers unique challenges and opportunities for journalists, particularly third places and incidental places.

Official spaces include such things as city council meetings where the formal business of politics and civic life occur. These are familiar and comfortable to most journalists, less well-known and comfortable for citizens.

Quasi-official spaces are such things as neighborhood associations, civic groups, and nonprofit, grassroots organizations in which meetings are held, leaders designated and agendas are prepared. Both journalists and citizens move fairly easily in those spaces.

Third places is the name given to public gathering places, rooted in daily life, where people choose to spend their free time: barbershops, churches, coffee shops, bookstores, recreation centers. These places are not expressly political, but conversation about challenges, concerns and ideas is common and informal.

The *incidental* layer of civic life results from random, everyday encounters among friends and acquaintances in which gossip, chitchat, storytelling

---

[10]Washington, D.C.: Pew Center for Civic Journalism, 2nd edition, April 2000.

and idea exchanges occur on sidewalks, front porches, in the school parking lot, at the soccer game. It is "the swamp" of public life.

Private spaces are inside the home where conversation is limited to those who live there.

As the objective of public listening is to hear real conversations not affected by the trappings of formality, the third place and incidental conversations are of the most interest and potential use for journalists. They are also the most difficult to access. The primary difficulty, but one that can be overcome, is that a journalist who goes into those places as a journalist immediately changes them. Going into those places in search of stories or quotes simply frustrates both the participants and the journalist and changes the nature of the conversations.

The Wichita, Kan., experiment involved reporters identifying third places in various parts of the city and going into them as committed observers interested in finding out how the people and places work and why people talk and believe as they do (as opposed to going in search of stories.) Succeeding at that obviously requires both time and good will, but the results can be important: a fuller, more intimate knowledge of the community and its people; a common perspective on events to balance the official perspective that most reportorial practice provides; insights into issues and concerns before they reach the official layer; and, importantly, a perception on the part of citizens that reporters and their institutions are honestly interested in them.

Reaping these benefits can require some trade-offs on the reporter's part. The notebook stays in the pocket and the camera is left at the office: The reporter is there to learn and understand, not to grab a quick story or a quote. Sometimes, particularly in the early stages of developing the rapport, reaping the long-term benefit means passing over a potential story in favor of learning things much more valuable. Good reporters do that with their normal, official sources, sometimes deciding that a continuing relationship built on mutual trust is more important over time than ripping off a small story.

Sometimes the reporter needs to become part of the conversation rather than merely acting as an observer to encourage and stimulate the conversation (without directing it) and to build trust and a human connection with the people there. Such participation does not violate the journalistic principle of not becoming a part of the story because reporters are not there to get a story. Reporters are there to learn about civic life in their community and use that to better inform their work. They are there to gain knowledge and insight, not information.

Another important advantage of moving in those third and incidental places is that the reporter learns who the leaders are in that segment of the community: the thought leaders who stimulate conversation and know what is going on. Those people, outside of those places, can be cultivated as sources of information, insights and ideas.

Harwood's framework helps to identify different types of leaders, including two types—catalysts and connectors—who, unlike elected leaders and civic leaders, are not usually known to reporters yet who play important roles in community life.

The publication *Tapping Civic Life* contains rich detail about how to take advantage of the process and turn it into better journalism.

CIVIC MAPPING AND THE SWAMP

Some newspapers and broadcast outlets, with help from the Pew Center and the Harwood Group, have taken the listening process a step further by experimenting in what is called "civic mapping." The origins of the concept lie in remarks made in 1993 by David Mathews, president of the Kettering Foundation of Dayton, Ohio.[11] He compared the most fundamental and essential processes of civic life to the swamps of his native South. The swamps, he said, were viewed for decades as places of little value, a region of snakes and 'gators, strange noises, mosquitos, and bad smells. When waterside property became scarce, it occurred to some people to fill in the swamps and build condominiums, shopping centers and housing developments, superimposing their notion of usefulness on what they felt was a useless, smelly mess.

Of course, the inevitable happened. The fish in the bays began to disappear, the shrimp became scarce and the water turned foul. A fundamental and microbiologically crucial process that humans could not see and would not have found very attractive had been going on in the swamp, and we had interfered with it. We began to learn the lessons of ecology.

Mathews drew the comparison with the cultural ecology of civic life that has a swamp of its own, a fundamental place where public issues first arise and brew in a conversational stewpot of opinion, rumor, fact and conjecture. It exists out of sight of journalists who are either ignorant of its importance or fastidious about its messiness and therefore avoid that cultural swamp. Instead, we as journalists focus coverage of public affairs on formal, safe, visible governmental and civic structures and easy-to-reach experts, superimposing our notions of public life on the reality of the swamp. This avoidance of or ignorance about the swamp creates two dangers for journalists: We don't really know what is going on, why issues are arising and how they move, and that lack of understanding leads us to reflect, in our reporting, a process of civic life that simply does not ring true with the people in the swamp. And it creates a danger for the cultural swamp itself, as, like the developers of the natural swamp, we run the risk, through our ignoring it or our lack of interest, of damaging the process itself and losing its benefits.

---

[11]David Mathews, speech to an American Press Institute seminar. Reston, VA, November 1993.

The Harwood idea is to make a map of that cultural swamp and help journalists learn how to operate within it without, as the developers did with Mathews' biological swamp, destroying it.

Rebecca Allen, an editor at *The Orange County Register,* helped lead about 100 members of that California newspaper's staff through the learning process in 1998 to 1999. The process was not an easy one and required commitment, she said, but immediately began to pay off because, "I began to see stories get better." Here's how she characterized her newspaper's venture into the swamp.

> When I was first introduced to the concepts of civic mapping, I was very put off by what seemed like a lot of empty jargon to me. It felt as if I was in a blizzard of *connectors, catalysts, essences* and *frames.* But I learned as we studied the concepts that they can be very helpful for journalists. I came to this realization when I started seeing stories get better. For example, the idea of *connectors* (people who connect and spread ideas and norms among various organizations or groups) in the community and *catalysts* (unofficial experts who spark change) is useful.
>
> For years we talked about officials and "real people" but reporters were reluctant to quote anyone without a title. Now it seems very clear that there are many people with vast amounts of knowledge and expertise on their neighborhoods or on an issue who should be in stories to help the reader understand and work through the issues.[12]

AN INFORMAL PROCESS

Listening differently need not involve a formal process, although both the learning curve and results are accelerated when the formal commitment is made. The key to better listening in either environment is, again, one of positioning on the part of the reporter. Traditional journalistic training, the dogma of the profession, insists that we as journalists act at all times as detached observers, as recorders of a passing scene. When we listen only from that position, we miss a great deal. Having a useful conversation aimed at discovery rather than reporting a specific story requires that we participate also as a citizen. The important content of such a conversation is often not in the questions we ask and the responses received so much as it is in the give-and-take, the sharing of thoughts and ideas.

Absent an organized process that involves many members of a staff, individuals can develop their own routines for listening in a different way. It may be as simple as deciding that you as a journalist will engage two or three people a week in a conversation aimed not at "getting news" but at gathering understanding. Initiating such conversations requires that the person being engaged believes that you value his or her words for their own sake and not as ammunition for some journalistic act.

---

[12]*Civic catalyst.* Washington, D.C.: Pew Center for Civic Journalism, Summer 1999, p. 12.

"I want to understand about. …"

"Tell me why you feel as you do about. …"

"Have you always felt that way, and if not, what changed your mind?"

"If you need something done in your neighborhood, who do you call? And who would he or she then call?"

"What things are you most concerned about?"

"What concerns you about that?"

"What are the arguments for the other side of the question?"

These are the kinds of questions that can lead to understanding.

All of the foregoing—the four values, the tools of positioning and public listening, understanding public judgment—will be essential as journalism seeks to define a more useful role for itself in the complex, relentlessly changing environment of 21st century democratic life. They are neither, however, a quick fix for public malaise nor an easy device for propping up stories. The objective of journalists positioning themselves to hear the public voice is two-fold: first, to make their stories more authentic and thus more resonant with readers, who can then begin to see themselves as a public capable of action; and second, to communicate those voices to decision makers and leaders.

Moving to this dual role completes the change of journalists from Lippmann's conduit between decision makers and from them to citizens by also making journalists conduits from citizens to decision makers and from citizens to other citizens.

Finding and communicating public voices does not guarantee, of course, that the voices will be immediately heard by those directly responsible for conducting the public's business. Often, in fact, rigidly structured government processes—public hearings, committee hearings, closed discussions by officials—fail to invite or recognize more than limited public participation. Worse, such processes do invite and recognize the voices of organized interests that have the time and resources to closely track government and political activities and influence them.

But, as readers will see, even the most arcane and distant processes (setting energy policy, for example) can be penetrated by public voices when media or academia or citizen groups combine relevant information with opportunity. The mechanism that organizes those voices is deliberation.

Suggestions for Additional Reading

Daniel Yankelovich, *"Coming to public judgment."* Syracuse, NY: Syracuse University Press, 1991.

Daniel Yankelovich, *"The magic of dialogue."* New York: Simon & Schuster, 1999.

The most common example of deliberation occurs in courtrooms. A jury of ordinary people is supplied, not coincidentally, with the same three elements that are required for democracy:

- Shared, relevant information: that is, facts that are found to be relevant through the process of give-and-take among the two sides and the judge.
- A forum for discussing the implications of those facts: the court process and the jury room.
- Shared values: the law as explained by the judge constitutes one set of values to be applied to the facts, although jurors certainly also bring their personal values to the deliberation.

Jurors are expected to carefully weigh the facts against the law, listen to the views of other jurors, evaluate the consequences of various courses of action, and make a decision they all can live with. They are not required to surrender deeply held values, however, and if they cannot, in due course, reach a decision, the process starts over with a new trial.

But deliberation is also common in other areas of everyday life. Decisions within families about buying a new home or car can have the qualities of deliberation; individual decisions about whether to marry, to take a new job, to undergo a medical treatment involve a careful weighing of choices and consequences and referring to core values.

So deliberation is a natural human instinct, at least when people are facing personal choices and referring to their own values or those of a family. It is not, however, the first and most natural instinct when people move into the public arena in which competing values are held by other people. Such occasions often begin in discussion or debate and, too often, end there. The difference, again, is a lack of agreed on, shared values. If, for instance, people involved in a debate over abortion policy can find a common ground or shared values, such as reducing the need for abortions in the first place, that debate can turn into deliberation—a quest for a joint course of action. Agreeing on the broad goal does not resolve the sticky questions of how to reach that goal, but a shared assumption that reducing abortions is in the public interest at least creates the possibility of progress rather than dictating unending debate.

In the area of public life and politics, rising from discussion and debate to the level of deliberative dialogue is sometimes difficult for a number of reasons, including:

- The presence of deeply held beliefs thought to be nonnegotiable.
- Lack of understanding or will or experience.
- Failure to grasp the importance of looking beyond one's particular interests to a broader public interest.
- The logistics of time and space.

Each of those hurdles is formidable, but each can yield to the right combination of incentives.

Deliberation, compared with discussion, debate and dialogue, has an additional dimension: It can be singular in that one can deliberate within oneself by applying the skills and principles of the more traditional process of group deliberation. It is a habit of mind that can be learned and its results applied in the public arena as well as in private decisions. In the private sense, deliberation moves from worrying about something to identifying and carefully analyzing alternatives and consequences. Private deliberation is not totally private, however, in the sense that it requires considering the consequences of an action for others as well as oneself; it involves some weighing of public interest. Only hermits, by choice, and misanthropes, by inclination, deliberate without regard for others.

DELIBERATION AND DEMOCRACY

Robert J. Kingston of the Kettering Foundation expressed the connection between deliberation and democracy this way:

> The quality of public life in the American democracy is in no small measure determined by the consistency with which we, citizens, deliberate on choices that confront us in facing the problems common to us as a people. ... We live somewhere *between* agreement and disagreement; problems that concern all of us do not concern all of us in precisely the same ways. There are, behind every public issue ... moral questions on which our judgments diverge. Not that we are poles apart on what is right or wrong, what is virtue and sin; but our senses of which is more important among competing needs, our priorities, are often at odds because we value particular aspects of experience (and particular human needs) somewhat differently. Deliberation, then, is the means by which we discover the public good—which is to say, that which may be good for us as a people, even if it is not what we see as ideally good for us or some others as individuals.[3]

So deliberation, as a habit of mind and action and in its various forms, can help to answer democracy's core question, "What shall we do?" Deliberation is not the only way the question can be answered, but it is a way that is reasoned and inclusive and far superior in a democratic context to decision making solely by elites or elected officials who, absent clear instruction from citizens, will act out of interests and values that may not necessarily reflect the public interest as determined through deliberation.

When one incorporates into the role of the journalist helping people engage in public life, it becomes apparent that deliberation is a concept that we as journalists should not only be familiar with but also an idea that should inform much of our thinking and writing. This raises an additional point of inquiry. If deliberation is a tool of democracy and potentially a tool of jour-

---

[3]Robert J. Kingston, Editor's letter, *The Kettering Review* (Fall 1999), pp. 4–5.

nalism, we need to identify its specific characteristics before we can apply them in our reporting and editing routines.

Amy Guthmann and Dennis Thompson, who wrote about deliberative democracy in *"Democracy and Disagreement,"* are helpful to our thinking about the characteristics of deliberation. They identified three conditions essential to true deliberation.

Reciprocity is the seeking of fair terms of social cooperation for their own sake to find mutually acceptable ways of resolving moral disagreements.[4]

Publicity argues that the reasons citizens and officials give for their positions should be public, partly to ensure that they are reciprocal but also to realize the value of openness.[5]

Accountability means that citizens and officials try to justify their decisions to all those who are bound by them and some of those who are affected by them.[6]

With these understandings of the nature and uses of deliberation, we look at examples of citizen deliberation and think about how journalism can be a catalyst to this essential democratic function.

NATIONAL ISSUES CONVENTION EXPERIMENT

When John Dewey and Walter Lippmann debated the nature of democracy and the role of citizens in it, they were extending an argument that has occupied democratic theorists for 2,000 years or more and continues today. The heart of the disagreement is whether ordinary citizens are capable of addressing tough political issues even when given the tools they need: relevant information and a method for discussing the implications of that information. Can ordinary citizens set aside their preconceptions and overcome their lack of factual knowledge to engage in serious deliberation? Will the deliberation lead to a different public judgment about those issues?

In January 1996, encouraging signs arose that they can. In that month, 466 perfectly ordinary and randomly chosen Americans gathered in Austin, Texas, for the National Issues Convention. Years of planning and more than $4 million went into the brainchild of political scientist James Fishkin of the University of Texas. Fishkin's objective was to demonstrate that what he called "deliberative polling" deserves an important place in the political and journalistic landscape. At the simplest level, deliberative polling involves asking peoples' opinion on public issues in advance, bringing them together

---

[4] Amy Guthmann and Dennis Thompson, *"Democracy and disagreement."* Cambridge, MA: Belknap Press of Harvard, 1996, pp. 52–53.

[5] Guthmann and Thompson, *"Democracy and disagreement,"* p. 95.

[6] Guthmann and Thompson, *"Democracy and disagreement,"* p. 128.

to deliberate about those issues then repeating the survey to see if their deliberations result in change.

The National Issues Convention was a complex event offering almost unlimited opportunities for research into people, politics, issues, values and processes, far too many to be dealt with here. The *"The Poll With A Human Face"* chronicles much of that research.[7] For our purposes in thinking about deliberation, we focus on the two previous questions: Can average people deliberate on serious issues and will that deliberation make any difference in their views of those issues? Would average people, given relevant information and a chance to reflect on that information with others, develop a different opinion on issues?

Putting together the Austin, Texas, gathering was a formidable and time-consuming task that began in November 1995 with interviewers from the National Opinion Research Center at the University of Chicago traveling to 387 neighborhoods around the country to conduct face-to-face surveys of attitudes and beliefs about three issues: foreign affairs, the economy and the family. Thirty-minute interviews were completed with 910 people. Following the interviews, the randomly chosen respondents were invited to attend the National Issues Convention the following January, all expenses paid and with a companion if desired. Put yourself in the place of a person who, having completed the survey, is faced with such a proposition from a complete stranger. Doubt, suspicion, and concern were rampant. Surely this was a scam or trap of some sort. In the next few weeks, however, National Opinion Research Center staffers managed to persuade 497 of the respondents to accept the offer and, of those, 466 actually made it to Austin.

There they were presented with briefing materials on the three issues. The materials were compiled by the nonpartisan, nonprofit National Issues Forum Network and Public Agenda, which worked with both major political parties and other competing sources to ensure that the information was accurate and balanced. The objective of the convention was not to try to reach consensus on the issues; it was to have the delegates frame questions on those issues to be asked of the presidential candidates during a televised national forum at the end of the weekend.

The delegates were randomly divided into groups of about 15 to engage in deliberations on the issues, aided by trained moderators from the National Issues Forum network. The scene was striking: a welfare mother sitting next to a retired businessman, who is next to a nursing mother, who is next to a rock band drummer with tattoos and green hair, who is next to a car salesman, who is next to a high school chemistry teacher, all there for the purpose of talking about public policy issues.

---

[7]Maxwell McCombs and Amy Reynolds, editors, *"The poll with a human face: The National Issues Convention experiment in political communication."* Mahwah, NJ: Lawrence Erlbaum Associates, 1999.

And talk they did, for hours. As is typical and necessary in deliberation, knee-jerk opinions, fondly held assumptions (and misconceptions) and misinformation emerged first. These were quickly challenged, as, for instance, when a remark about welfare mothers was greeted with, "Yes, that's me," from the person in the next chair. Second thoughts began to emerge, as people actually faced the flesh-and-blood embodiments of the images and assumptions in their heads.

Facts were brought to bear on misinformation. A statement such as, "We could solve the problems of education if we wouldn't spend all that money on foreign aid" was faced with the budget reality that foreign aid is less than 2 percent of federal spending, hardly enough to "fix" public education.

At the end of the convention, the delegates were given the same opinion survey they had responded to three months earlier. Had their discussions changed anything? Yes. The delegates' attitude, knowledge and opinions all changed at statistically significant levels on a number of key items. In describing their own roles, delegates were more likely to agree with the statement "I have worthy political opinions" after the convention than before. Likewise, fewer agreed with the statements, "I have no say in government," and "politicians are out of touch." Not surprisingly, because they were given factual information, delegates' knowledge about the issues improved. Perhaps most significantly, their opinions on several parts of the three issues changed in statistically significant ways.[8]

The National Issues Convention experiment thus demonstrates that deliberation is a tool for developing sounder, more thoughtful public judgments and that average citizens are capable of participating at a high level given the resources and the opportunity. The National Issues Convention did not, of course, reflect the real world of public life and politics. It was a limited demonstration of deliberation. The process we think about next moves citizen deliberation a step closer to that real world.

NATIONAL ISSUES FORUMS

The idea of people getting together to address the question, "What shall we do?" is rooted in the concept of democracy and has found various forms of expression over the centuries, from the early Greek republics to the town meetings of the colonial United States. Its forms reflect the practicalities of the times, but the objective remains constant: seeking common ground for resolving public issues.

In "Politics for people," David Mathews described the development, over nearly two decades, of one broad-based process of deliberation: National Is-

---

[8]Complete statistical details are available in McCombs and Reynolds, "The poll with a human face," Chapters 1 and 2.

sues Forums that began in 1981 when several civic and educational organizations began to coordinate their efforts under the National Issues Forums umbrella. They annually take on three policy questions—such as crime or drugs or health care.

The Kettering Foundation and Public Agenda, another nonpartisan research organization, prepare issues books providing relevant, shared information. As Mathews explained it:

> When institutions began holding NIF discussions, they shared one central objective: they were decidedly not interested in just making improvements in what they were already doing—providing informative discussions. They wanted to develop a different type of public forum, one that would deal with issues from the public's perspective. That meant going behind technical, ideological, and legislative positions to find out how each issue affects what is most valuable to people. Issues are then re-framed into three or four options that capture these "values" or deeper motivations that are at play. The issue books spell out the consequences of each alternative approach. Participants in the forums do the difficult work of deliberation—of moving toward a choice on each issue by weighing carefully the pros and cons of every option. The premise is that the pulls and tugs of having to make choices together will cause people to learn more about policy issues and move from individual opinions toward more shared and reflective judgments. The objectives of the forums are to help people become a public, to develop the skills needed for public politics, to speak in a public voice, and to contribute to defining the public's interests.[9]

Why is "creating a public voice" so important? Mathews explained it this way:

> Democratic governments need broad public support if they are to act consistently over the long term. … Governments can build common highways for us, but not common ground. And governments—even the most powerful—cannot provide the popular will needed for effective political action. Governments can command obedience, but they cannot create will. Finally, it is up to the public to transform private individuals into public citizens, people who are political actors. Citizens can create governments, but governments cannot create citizens. Only citizens can do that.[10]

ENOUGH ABOUT TALK, WHAT ABOUT POWER?

How do the ideas of representative government and centralized power square with the idea of citizen deliberation? How does the public voice, once organized, get heard through the wall of static thrown up around government and other institutions by special interests, hidden persuaders and money providers?

---

[9]Mathews, "*Politics for people*," p. 108.
[10]Mathews, "*Politics for people*," p. 110.

Political scientist Benjamin R. Barber raised the question pointedly in an essay for *The Kettering Review.*

> Deliberation without power is a fraud, and will soon burn out those compelled to talk without being able to make relevant decisions. Just as power without deliberation is despotism, even when it wears the cloak of representative democracy. Too many Americans have given up on voting, in many cases out of frustration, anger, and re-sentment—a sense that it just doesn't make a difference.

> Many more will give up on deliberation if they see it's only talk, venting feelings and opinions that will never touch the conduct of public affairs.... Forums on public issues have always faced this dilemma: fashioning remarkably competent conversation around complex policy issues and getting citizens to reach intelligent consensus on some possible policy solutions, but without being able to move to the action stage. Yet the challenge of full-blown democratic deliberation is how to turn a conversation that brings us to the edge of the water into a process that allows us to get our feet wet in the deep pool of real power.[11]

Although it's true that public deliberation does not often or automatically directly push the levers of policy, Barber's description of it as a zero-sum game is challenged by those deeply involved in encouraging deliberation and also by history.

Processes such as National Issues Forums help accumulate public judg-ment, and that public judgment is what, finally, informs, directs and legiti-mizes governments over the long term. That is surely a form of power, albeit latent. In isolation, deliberative forums can be frustrating and seem futile, as the connection between citizen deliberation and government-institutional power is hard to see in the short term to midterm.

But affecting government action is only one potential result of public deliberation. Another objective, perhaps a more important one, is that public deliberation can identify directions for actions that citizens can take, individually and in association with others, that do not depend on pushing the levers of government for their success. Think back to the ear-lier idea about journalists positioning themselves in the democratic equation. If there is a public voice, how can it be heard by those in power and thus transformed into power unless journalists themselves hear it and aid in its transmission? Journalists with both ears directed only to government, journalists who see themselves as one-way conduits from officialdom to the public, cannot help. Journalists with one ear to the sound of public voices are positioned to play a broader role than mere conduit and to help bring alive the latent power of deliberation both on government and outside of it.

---

[11]Benjamin R. Barber, Deliberation, democracy and power, *The Kettering Review* (Fall 1999), pp. 31–36.

FINDING THE PUBLIC VOICE

A striking example of how listening for the public voice and engaging citizens in deliberation can command power and cause action occurred in Charlotte, N.C., in 1994 to 1995 when that city was struggling with the nation's 18th highest crime rate. *The Charlotte Observer*, under the leadership of editor Jennie Buckner, decided extraordinary action was required beyond the daily and weekly telling of the story of crime.

Here is how the Charlotte story was told by Arthur Charity in "*Doing Public Journalism*:"

> What if instead (of simply narrating the news) the paper could get the whole city mobilized on behalf of the most troubled neighborhoods? "We would invite readers to help these neighborhoods help themselves. There would be no question but that we were all in this together, working to understand what to do about the problem" (Buckner said). ... The paper launched "Taking Back Our Neighborhoods," a one-and-one-half year project that would focus all of Charlotte's attention on ten target areas, each for six weeks at a time.[12]

After a June 5 exploration of the city's crime problem in broad terms, the first area targeted was Seversville. Reporters met with neighborhood leaders who told them about problems of crack cocaine, unemployment and stressed families. Building on those insights, *The Observer* developed an investigative series on the linkage between crack houses and absentee landlords and organized a community meeting to allow residents to talk about the problem. At a United Way resource fair after the meeting, scores of Seversville people signed up for neighborhood crime watches, Big Brothers programs and other United Way activities.

> The project's real test came on July 17, when the paper and its radio and TV partners introduced the entire city to Seversville, its problems and struggles, in a day-long media blitz. The coverage included an itemized list of needs in the neighborhood. By September, more than 200 organizations, individuals and agencies—from private firms to the YMCA—had offered their support, answering virtually every need on the list. ... The mayor and police stepped up city programs to complement the private activity.[13]

With that underway, the paper moved to its next target neighborhood with a different set of problems.

---

[12]Arthur Charity, "*Doing public journalism*." New York: Guilford Press, 1995, p. 134. Also see Edward D. Miller, "*The Charlotte project: Helping citizens take back democracy*." St. Petersburg, FL: Poynter Institute for Media Studies, 1994, which is still available.

[13]Charity, "*Doing public journalism*," p. 135.

Throughout the life of the project, civic forces responded and, perhaps more important, residents of the various neighborhoods came to understand that they could in fact affect their circumstances through the right kind of talk directed toward action. Importantly, the journalists at *The Observer* did not try to solve problems; they helped organize the latent ability and resources within the community for people to attack the problems. Recall the four obstacles to deliberation listed earlier. Each of those obstacles can, in fact, be made to yield the following:

- The presence of deeply held core values believed to be nonnegotiable.
- Lack of understanding or will or experience.
- Failure to grasp the importance of looking beyond one's particular interests to a broader public interest.
- The logistics of time and space.

In the Charlotte, N.C., case, the newspaper and broadcast stations brought to bear on a severe community problem activity that overcame several of those hurdles. They managed the logistical problem with the help of foundations and community institutions and provided for community forums. They demonstrated, in their reporting and through the forums the broad public interest that lay beneath, the problem of dangerous neighborhoods. The deliberations that they stimulated resulted in definitive action. The process did not rid the city of crime and it did not solve the myriad socio-economic problems that led to the troubles. But things got substantially better and the residents of the neighborhoods and Charlotte at large discovered that broad citizen engagement in talking about and acting on problems makes a difference. The neighborhoods and the community began to accumulate civic capital, including the recognition that power resides not only in official places and people but also in the public voice when it is organized and heard.

An experiment in Texas that combined deliberation and polling techniques provides an example of how citizen voices can be translated into direct impact on a government function.[14] Political scientist James Fishkin, developer of deliberative polling and organizer of the National Issues Convention described previously, worked with the Texas Public Utilities Commission, which requires that utilities allow the public to participate in developing "integrated resource plans" for how they will supply electricity. The utilities are charged with allocating resources among new fossil fuel plants, renewable energy such as wind and solar power, conservation efforts, and buying power from outside.

It would be of limited value to simply ask the public—in a poll or public meeting—for its guidance because making that allocation involves a level of technical and economic knowledge that most people simply don't posses.

---

[14]McCombs and Reynolds, *"The poll with a human face,"* pp. 32–36.

So Fishkin and his staff applied deliberative polling techniques to the problem. They drew representative samples of people within each utility's service area, provided them with balanced briefing materials dealing with the environmental and economic trade-offs involved in each choice, and brought them together for a weekend of deliberation. Care was taken that the sample was truly representative of various stakeholder groups—environmentalists, industry and consumers.

As with the National Issues Convention, and typical of deliberative polling protocol, the participants were polled in advance about their opinions and again after their deliberations. As with the National Issues Convention, minds were changed. In the first three distinct sessions, participants came in with a heavy bias toward renewable energy: It was the "first choice" among the four sources of at least two-thirds of them. During the deliberations, they learned more about the complexities of solar and wind as the primary source of power and their "first choice" shifted dramatically to conservation techniques as the most promising answer. They continued to think of renewable resources as an important part of the total package but decided that conservation serves as many of the environmental ends as wind and solar and does it more cost effectively. They said as much to the utilities.

As a result, the "Integrated Resource Plans" for all three utilities called for substantial investment in renewable sources but also put heavy emphasis on conservation education and techniques. Had the utilities tried to meet their requirement with only a poll, or only town meetings or focus groups—none of which involves deliberative techniques—they would have been faced with a public outcry for emphasis on renewables, which experts recognize as unreliable and not cost effective on a major scale. So the public voice was heard, but it was not an under informed or knee-jerk voice; it was one tempered by deliberation.

THE END GAME FOR JOURNALISTS

We have shown how deliberation and the public voice operate in the special circumstances of the National Issues Convention, within National Issues Forum deliberations, for a community that decides to face squarely its problems, and for a government agency that seeks input from citizens. All four of those circumstances demonstrate that citizens, given the information and opportunity, can think and act in the public interest as well as in their own interests. This is a piece of good news that is repeated over and over again across the nation in many different ways, but well below the conventional radar of news organizations.

Journalists interested in covering public affairs in this new century need, at a minimum, expanded radar capability that recognizes citizen engagement as important news. Beyond that minimum threshold lies the real opportunity. By understanding the principles and potential effect of a deliberative democracy and a deliberative mindset, journalists covering public affairs can do their jobs in ways that encourage deliberation and begin to accumulate and empower the public voice.

Suggestions for Additional Reading

Maxwell McCombs and Amy Reynolds,(Eds.)., *The poll with a human face: The National Issues Convention experiment in political communication.* Mahwah, NJ: Lawrence Erlbaum Associates, 1999.

David "Buzz" Merritt, *Public journalism and public life: Why telling the news is not enough, 2nd edition.* Mahwah, NJ: Lawrence Erlbaum Associates, 1998.

13

Elections

Fifty or a hundred years from now will Americans look back to turn-of-the-century elections and shake their heads in bewilderment, as people do today when they read about the electoral process as it existed in the mid-19th century? Will they wonder how democracy survived the days in the 1990s when presidential candidates spent more than $3 for every vote cast and U.S. senators had to raise thousands of dollars a day every day of their 6-year terms to compete for re-election? Will it seem a bizarre irony to those future historians that as more and more money was spent, fewer and fewer voters participated; that the White House was turned into a grand resort for major campaign contributors; that the major communication about candidates and issues was through 30-second sound bites on radio and television, where attack advertising dominated?

Will those scenes strike their sensibilities as harshly as Michael Schudson's description of Election Day in the middle of the 19th century strikes ours?

The area (around the polling place) is crowded with the banners and torches of rival parties. Election Day is not set off from other days but is the culmination of a campaign of several months. You must still be a white male to vote, but not necessarily of property. During the campaign you have marched in torchlight processions, perhaps in military uniform, with a club of like-minded individuals from your party . If you were not active in the campaign, you may be roused on election day by a party worker to escort you to the polls on foot or by carriage. On the road you may encounter clubs or groups from rival parties, and it would not be unusual if fisticuffs or even guns were to dissuade you from casting a ballot at all.

If you do proceed to the ballot box, you may step more lively with the encouragement of a dollar or two from the party—not a bribe but an acknowledgment that voting is a service to the party. A party worker hands you a "ticket" with the printed names of the party's candidates. The ticket is likely to be distinctive enough in shape and size that the poll watchers can readily see what party you vote as you place the ticket in the ballot box.[1]

The dust cover of Schudson's book, "*The Good Citizen*," shows Missouri artist and politician George Caleb Bingham's colorful painting of a mid-19th-century polling place bustling with activity: party workers vying to thrust those telltale tickets into voters' hands, a table where encouraging spirits are poured from oak barrels and knots of men engaged in energetic conversations while a party member supports a clearly drunken citizen toward his civic duty of voting. To our eyes, the scene is one of chaos and corruption. To citizens of the day, it was the business of political life.

Surely, we believe looking back, a free democracy could not have long survived such a process, and indeed, reform followed in the early 20th century with the adoption of the secret, government-issued ballot and limits on party activities, at least at the polling places.

Will those future observers be enjoying a less corrupt, more accessible process than we have now because of 21st century reforms yet to be accomplished? And if not, who should be held accountable for that failure? At least some of the responsibility must be borne by journalists, who have become a tightly integrated part of the electoral process as we know it. Indeed, some critics argue that the news media are at the core of the problems of early 21st century politics and that the process cannot change unless journalists change. Although one can debate the degree to which that charge is fair or accurate, there is no question that the way journalists do their jobs has major impact on the process.

That being the case, it's important to think about how that work is done and how it might be done differently.

SCENE ONE

The Republican delegates are gathering in San Diego in the summer of 1996 to formally nominate Sen. Bob Dole as their candidate, the nomination having been decided months before via the extensive primary election system. Journalists outnumber the delegates by 4-to-1 for the week-long gathering. But one notable journalist leaves after the first day. Ted Koppel, host of the popular "Nightline" show and one of America's most respected broadcasters, bolts from the city, taking his crew and declaring, "There's no news here."

---

[1]Schudson, "*The good citizen*," p. 5.

Just what did that complaint mean? The convention was going to be held, a party platform would be adopted, Dole and others would make speeches outlining their hopes and dreams for the nation, and a vice-presidential candidate would be selected and the fall campaign launched. Did Koppel mean by "no news here" that surprises, conflict and intrigue would be lacking? In a broader sense, was he reaffirming not only that pinched definition of news, but was he also reaffirming that the journalist's role ends with telling news and entertaining people?

What if Koppel and other broadcast journalists decided that they had a broader purpose in addition to telling news. If, for instance, Americans could look at political television—such as a national party convention—not only as a way of being informed but also a way of becoming engaged; and if political reporting could begin where citizens begin and not where politicians and journalists begin; if the focus of convention coverage could be on telling Americans about how the convention is addressing the nation's problems rather than how it is addressing the party's tactical problems as defined by politicians and journalists, then audiences would have an incentive to pay attention and democracy a chance to be refreshed. And Ted Koppel could have stayed around.

SCENE TWO

Texas Gov. George W. Bush has just swept all the Republican delegates available on Super Tuesday 2000, ending Sen. John McCain's insurgency against the party establishment, which has backed Bush almost from the beginning with big money and early endorsements. Meanwhile, Vice President Al Gore has seemingly disposed of his only rival, Bill Bradley, in the Democratic primaries. Bradley gracefully bows out, formally ending his campaign. McCain "suspends" his campaign without formally dismantling it. It is only the first week in March and the intraparty campaigns are suddenly, and for journalists distressingly, over. The nominating conventions are not until July and the election not until November, so suddenly the airwaves and Web sites are full of talk about a McCain third-party bid, never mind that McCain has never hinted in any way that he would be interested in such a historically futile move. But because he only suspended his campaign and it looked, otherwise, as if the party was over as far as the broadcasters were concerned, or at least in deadly suspension for four-to-eight months, they filled at least some of all that airtime devoted to the 2000 campaign speculating about the possibility of a third-party effort.

SCENE THREE

For the 1996 congressional elections, most of the larger newspapers in North Carolina joined in a cooperative venture aimed at engaging citizens more directly in the electoral process. They pooled resources to carry out extensive, statewide surveys to discover what issues citizens felt the candidates for various offices should address. They then shared material built around those issues and bombarded the candidates with questions aimed at getting them to address those issues. This was done in addition to the newspapers' normal, independent campaign coverage, with the objective of reinvigorating the role of citizens in a process that, in recent elections, had shut them out. Strangely, the experiment was roundly criticized by the established political press. Within three weeks, just before election day, *The Washington Post, The New York Times, The Boston Globe* and *New Yorker* magazine all printed scathing critiques, labeling the cooperative as "fraud," "manipulative" and "dishonest." Staffers of the North Carolina coalition papers found it difficult to understand how asking voters what issues they wanted the candidates to address could approach anything like fraud or manipulation. It is interesting that the sources those elite publications interviewed as backgrounding for their critical stories were all politicians or campaign handlers. Most of the complaints from the campaigns had to do with their inability to control events and the content of the reporting.

Revealingly, in no case did the people writing the critical stories ask any North Carolina citizen for an opinion of the effort, which clearly raises several questions:

- Why did the established political press not ask any citizens whether they were benefitting from the information they were getting?
- Who owns the electoral process anyway? Is it the closed preserve of candidates, handlers and the political press, with citizens relegated to the role of spectator up until election day itself?
- Who, after all, are the largest stakeholders in that process, candidates and the media? Or do citizens actually have the most at stake in the process as well as the outcome?

Ample evidence exists—from surveys and the analysis of voter turnout—that the more citizens are treated as only spectators (or worse, the objects of manipulation) during the weeks leading up to an election, the fewer bother to vote and the less stake they feel they have in the government that results from the election.

If democracy is going to function effectively, this disconnect between citizens and the process needs to be healed. Journalists play a central role in creating the disconnect and thus, by rethinking our practices, journalists can play a central role in putting the process back together. The electoral process boils down to three main groups of participants: the candidates and their handlers, the news media, and citizens—the potential voters. Each has a distinctive place and distinctive objectives.

Campaigners have no incentive to change the way it is being done. Over recent decades, the planning and execution of political campaigns has become a large and lucrative industry with specialists in research, spin control, strategy and tactics, fund raising, advertising and, unfortunately, attack approaches. Campaigners have a large stake in keeping the process as it is. As Jay Rosen pointed out, when the campaign gets ugly, the specialized handlers are needed even more. Here's how he described that aspect of modern political campaigns:

> Delta (airlines) would never dream of saying in advertisements, "Sure, fly the risky skies of United. ... " Though it is no less driven to dominate the field and vanquish competitors, a major airline would not try to raise doubts about safety, for the simple reason that public trust in the industry as a whole is invaluable to each enterprise in that industry.
>
> Mutually assured destruction, a cold war threat, can seem rational in the election industry only because costs that come with the pattern are not borne by the key players. If, (in the airline industry) through a savage campaign against competitors, you hike market share but lose half the market to auto and train travel, you are later fired from Delta. In politics, you're a winner. ... The key players who profit—consultants, pollsters, media wizards, ad makers, funders, handlers and assorted professionals—accrue an investment in the "it's gonna get ugly" style of realism. If it gets ugly, candidates (and reporters) need these people more.[2]

Rosen's apt analogy is both instructive and disturbing. Delta knows that it cannot reasonably expect to own the entire market and so has an incentive to protect not only its share but also the total market. Political operatives, however, see elections as a zero-sum game, winner take all, and apparently do not envision the larger stakes in "the entire market," that is, the democratic process. This is wrong-headed. So campaigns have little incentive to change. The objective is to win at any cost—even at the cost of the ability of the victor to govern from strength.

Citizens, positioned by the campaigns and the news media outside the process, have no ready way to change either themselves or the process, even if they had an incentive.

Journalists, on the other hand, have both the incentive and the ability to change. The incentive for journalists to change is twofold: Citizens who are increasingly frustrated by and withdrawn from public life have increasingly less use for any journalistic product; and journalism most certainly has a large stake in the preservation of democracy, which is both its lifeblood and its reason for existing.

REFORMING ELECTORAL COVERAGE

The objective of reforming electoral coverage is to move its primary focus away from the politicians and the process and onto citizens; to start the cover-

---

[2]*http://www.Speakout.com/activism/opinions/5086-1.html* Retrieved 5/3/03.

age where citizens start. In the words of Jay Rosen, this requires adopting a different "master narrative" or frame. In politics, that master narrative—the thought that drives all else—is winning. As Rosen wrote, "A narrative frame is something set prior to the story, in part because it consists of assumptions that tell journalists where a good story is to be found. ... master narratives hand out assigned roles."[3] Another commentator on traditional journalistic practice, former *Washington Post* reporter Paul Taylor, pointed out that, "Political stories do not just 'happen' the way hailstorms do. They are artifacts of a political universe that journalism itself has helped construct."[4]

What different master narrative might journalists help to construct? Is winning as the master narrative of political campaigns—and coverage—sufficient for an effective democracy that engages citizens? We think not, for after winning must come governing, and while winning is largely the concern of politicians and campaigns, governing is the primary concern of citizens.

This first step toward recognizing a new master narrative is to establish a clear distinction in our minds between the two separate things that are going on during a voting season: the campaign and the election.

The campaign is the task that politicians and their handlers face: the challenge of winning votes. Their plans for doing that are based in how they can control the discussion so that their candidates' strengths are shown and their weaknesses hidden, and the opposite for their opponents. They decide, within that context, what issues they will talk about and what issues they will not address. They decide the circumstances in which that will happen, the timing of various media events, and conjure with how they can attract attention from the press when they want it and avoid it when they don't want it. That's their job, and it is about control.

The election is the job that citizens face: to choose. The verb is from the Latin *electus,* or choice, and it is useful and important to think of the election as a verb, an action, and not a noun, an event. Citizens are not merely choosing people to win or lose, they are choosing people to entrust with governing. If the campaign is so destructive and divisive that the winners cannot govern, what has been gained?

For decades, the focus of news media coverage has been on the campaign, the horse race, with all its polarization, machinations, gaffes and scandals. Reporters follow the candidates around, write about what they do and say, ask questions about tactics and plans, and analyze the strategy of the campaign. It's largely an interaction between the press and the campaign. In this mode, voters are positioned as objects being acted on by a combination of the media and the campaigns. That's how the campaigns like to position them; but that's not how citizens position themselves, nor should journalists position them that way.

---

[3]Jay Rosen, personal communication. "*I say it often.*" March 2001

[4]Quoted in Rosen, "*What are journalists for?,*" p. 235.

Shifting the Emphasis

Turning the primary focus onto the job citizens face does not mean ignoring the campaign, but it does require fundamental shifts in emphasis to make sure that we as journalists are paying at least as much attention to the task that faces voters as we are to the task that faces the candidates and their handlers. Those mental and practical shifts include the following:

Recognizing that the electoral process should begin with what citizens need to have to carry out their job of choosing. This implies discovering early on what concerns citizens have, what issues they want the future officeholders to address, and developing a plan to ensure that those issues are in fact addressed by the candidates.

A classic example of how a determined and well-executed plan can affect the campaign process arose in North Carolina in 1992. *The Charlotte Observer* surveyed citizens about their concerns, and the environment was among the top ones listed. *The Observer* developed an "issues box" around those concerns during the primary campaign and asked the candidates for the U.S. Senate to say what they would do about them. The staff for one candidate, incumbent Sen. Terry Sanford, responded that within its strategy, "the senator doesn't plan to address the environment during the primary." *The Observer* editor Rich Oppel didn't accept that response. The citizens who had been surveyed wanted to know the senator's position before the primary, not afterward. It was a clear example of a disconnect between what citizens needed and what the campaign felt it needed to do. Who would prevail? Oppel reached the senator himself and received the same answer: "We aren't going to talk about that now." Fine, Oppel responded, when we print our issues box about the candidates' environmental positions, it will include your picture and a blank space beneath it. The senator's campaign quickly provided the senator's position.

Accepting the responsibility of actively framing those issues from the citizens' perspective rather than passively accepting the frames established by the candidates. E. J. Dionne Jr., in his important book, *"Why Americans Hate Politics,"* pointed out that politicians tend to frame issues at the extremes so as to create clear differences from their rivals' positions. As the rhetoric of the campaign mounts, the rivals' positions are driven further and further apart. This often artificial polarization can distort the issues beyond recognition and reality. Perversely, the polarization is self-perpetuating, as both the news media and opponents are quick to label a candidate's attempt to modify a position as "waffling" or "being soft," a label few candidates are willing to invite. Yet there are many reasons why modifying a position might be both wise and ethical: changed circumstances, new information, intellectual growth and, even, a genuine desire to compromise.

Worse, however, is the impact such polarized issue framing has on citizens. Most people on most issues harbor some level of ambiguity, and when the issues are framed as polar A and Z, people do not see themselves as part of the discussion because their often more moderate views are not reflected. The clear message to citizens of issue polarization is, "This isn't about what you think of the issue; you're not part of this discussion." Citizens turn away in frustration or disgust. If it's true, as Dionne suggested, that Americans hate politics, journalists must ask themselves, "Where do these Americans who hate politics learn most of what they know about the politics they hate?" And the answer is obvious: from journalists. It is not the job of journalists to try to make Americans love politics, but it is certainly our job to ensure that citizens are included in the process, and issue framing is a major part of that responsibility.

If coverage of a campaign debate on an issue focuses exclusively on the polarized framing provided by the candidates, the job of reporting on that issue (as opposed to merely reporting on the argument between the candidates) is only half done. If the issue exists because it is important to people's lives, not simply because it is important to the candidates' campaigns, then the journalistic responsibility is to frame the issue in its fullness, not merely at the polar extremes. This means understanding and pointing out the whole array of possible solutions, not simply the two conflicting ones proposed by the opponents, and asking the opponents to talk about areas of the problem on which they agree in addition to asking them about areas on which they disagree.

Treating the electoral process as a deliberative one—responsible voters deliberate—rather than a debating contest in which journalists are merely the scorekeepers assigned to tell people who is ahead and who is behind. This is where the two factors just mentioned—discovering citizen concerns and framing the issues broadly—are brought together and journalism begins to play a part that is more useful than a narrowly defined reportorial and scorekeeping role. To illustrate the possibilities, assume that your news operation has discovered from its surveys that an important concern of voters in an election for county commissioner is what to do about trash. The background is this: the county's landfill is full and the federal Environmental Protection Agency has ordered it closed in 5 years. The choice—how to manage the area's solid waste in the future—is not a simple one. The most obvious alternatives include building a new landfill, using transfer stations to package the waste to be trucked to a regional landfill in another county, and building an incinerator to burn the trash. Each choice has obvious environmental, political and fiscal implications. Because of an existing split on the county commission, the winner of this seat will have the swing vote on the choice.

In this hypothetical election campaign, Gerald Smith, the Democrat, insists that a new landfill is the best, most environmentally sound solution and is prepared to vote to build it on land already owned by the county, overriding the protests of the people who live in the area. Anne Johnson, the Republican, favors a transfer system whereby the trash would be assembled at three centers and trucked to a regional landfill in another county. They have been debating the issue for weeks, and at times the dispute has grown bitter. Smith has accused Johnson of being in the pocket of the commercial trash company that serves the area and also operates the regional landfill that would receive the trash, and in fact, the company was a major contributor to Johnson's campaign. For her part, Johnson argues that Smith has no regard for the property values and sensibilities of the people who live around the proposed new landfill, which will clearly have a negative impact on the area. Residents of the area have been loudly insistent that Smith represents the heavy, uncaring hand of government that will destroy their lives and devalue their property.

Your news operation has been covering that argument since it first began in the primary election, and now it is the centerpiece of the runoff campaign. Your surveys show that the main concern citizens have is the environmental impact of whatever method is chosen. Cost, they say, is important but secondary because the landfill and the transfer station are about equal in cost. A new incinerator would come at a very high initial cost, but if it works well would, in the long run, be the most cost-efficient.

Much of the debate between the rivals has centered on cost. And, as typical in such situations, the sides are dealing with different sets of numbers. Average citizens do not have the expertise to sort out the truth of the numbers, and each side has a compelling argument for and experts to back up its figures. And, at any rate, the two costs are not far apart.

Who is right? Who knows, so far as the competing cost figures are concerned. That means voters must base their choice on other factors: who they trust personally, party affiliation, personality, the nature of the campaigns, a hunch perhaps, or throw up their hands and not vote at all.

This is an opportunity for a newspaper or broadcast outlet to reframe the debate to give people another, more sound basis on which to choose. Our news operation can do this by beginning where the citizens begin. Our surveys show that the relatively minor differences in cost are less valued by most citizens than the environment. That's where they begin.

So as a news operation we ask ourselves this question: What are the elements that add up to that overall environmental concern? We can do this in several ways:

- **We can contact an array of individual citizens and probe beyond the question, "Which proposal (or candidate) do you favor?"** These are more conversations than interviews, for we are not looking for quotes to include in a story; we are not trying to quantify sentiment. Rather, we are trying to discover the array of underlying values that constitute the overall environmental concern.
- **We can convene focus groups for moderated discussions of the issue, again not to produce stories or quantify support or try to reach a decision, but to discover values and possible common ground.**
- **We can do a survey aimed at discovering those values.**
- **We can hold a discussion among the reporters and editors most knowledgeable about the situation to try to articulate the values that lie beneath both proposals.**

Having done one or more of those things, we then are prepared to reframe the discussion along the lines of core values. One effective way of presenting this is through a "values exercise," which is far more dynamic and interesting than the name suggests.

In this exercise, our news operation articulates value choices and pairs them with the outcomes they suggest. Readers or viewers are then asked to think about the choices in terms of their own values. For example, if an important value to the reader is that a community take responsibility for its own trash rather than ship it to another community, that person would tend to favor the landfill. Readers who feel uncomfortable imposing a new landfill on fellow citizens would tend to favor the transfer stations. A reader whose environmental concern is primarily local, would tend to favor the transfer station. But if that environmental concern were broader and included the nearby county and its citizens, the reader might favor paying the higher immediate cost of an incinerator. Other tough choices can be illuminated by thinking of them as value trade-offs. For instance, under the transfer-station plan, three neighborhoods will be affected by truck traffic, noise and the other factors associated with transfer operations, whereas the landfill will disrupt only one neighborhood, albeit more dramatically than the three transfer stations. It is more than a political consideration. Where do the reader's personal values lie?

The exercise also has the advantage of allowing people to consider values that compete with theirs, a central element in deliberation.

We have thus re-framed the debate in a way that has resonance with citizens. We know that citizens facing difficult choices almost always fall back on their personal values, but they often do so almost unconsciously and without considering that others may hold competing values. This device surfaces all those values and makes the choices more conscious and considered. The values-exercise approach does more than help with this decision; it builds deliberative skills within the community.

Constantly asking ourselves this question: As a voter, am I finding out from our coverage what I need to know about what the candidate intends to do once in office?   Too often, campaign coverage revolves around what candidates think about issues as opposed to what they intend to do about them, around how they talk about issues rather than whether they have firm plans to deal with them. To get around this roadblock, it is useful for journalists to put themselves in the role of citizen, although that is difficult for many to do. Some journalists even insist that they do not—and should not—vote, arguing that participation would somehow diminish their objectivity or call it into question. But journalists who cannot place themselves in the additional role of citizen are bound to miss opportunities to serve the very citizens from whom they have distanced themselves. At such a distance, it is impossible to hear the voices of the people they are supposed to serve.

Asking ourselves, and inviting citizens to ask, "Would I hire this candidate for an important job?"   It is startling how framing the question that way dramatically changes the electoral environment. Suddenly personality becomes secondary to competence; track record overwhelms glibness; trust rises above almost all other factors, including party. We begin to consider factors we have not previously thought about. A number of newspapers have framed their election coverage in terms of a job application: Do I know enough about the candidates to make the decision to hire one of them to work for me at the job he or she is seeking? Thinking of the election in this way invites consideration in detail of what the job requires in the way of skills and experience and matching the candidates' background and personality to those.

OTHER TOOLS

These are some additional ways that news operations can help repair the disconnect between citizens and campaigns:

- Develop issues boxes, which are grids listing the primary issues in a contest, including those news operations identify from their research with citizens, and stating the candidates' stands on those issues. Some newspapers allow the campaigns to state the positions, while others have their reporters do it based on their coverage. On the key issues, it is important to present this more than once for at least two reasons: The positions sometimes shift subtly in ways that candidates would rather not acknowledge (which argues for reporters to state them) and not every person is paying attention on a given day.

- Develop issues stories framed in terms of competing core values and choices and consequences, as illustrated by the landfill example, rather than simply what the candidates are saying about the issues.
- Constantly provide activating information: where the candidates can be seen and heard, constant information on registration deadlines and voting procedures (early voting, absentee voting, etc.) and how to contact the campaigns.
- Solicit questions for the candidates from voters and other real people. Comparing the first five or six questions put to a candidate by reporters at any press conference with the first five or six questions put to them by citizens in a public forum setting reveals enormous differences. Most reporters' questions have to do with tactics and the horse race; most voters' questions have to do with issues that concern them.
- Frame questions and analyze issue positions in terms of their impact on citizens as well as their impact on the horse race. ("What impact will your position on welfare have on people?," in addition to, "How will your position help you win?")
- Create campaign ad watches: graphics-oriented pieces that analyze campaign advertising on the basis of accuracy and how (or whether) the candidates are addressing the issues. Given the importance of advertising in today's campaigns, some newspapers also analyze ads from the point of view of the strategy they represent. That's useful if the newspapers have the resources to allow that in addition to "truth-squading" the ads. But dealing with distorted and misleading claims takes first priority.
- Regularly report on where the money comes from and where it goes.

STICK BY YOUR GUNS

Candidates and their handlers tend not to be pleased when the focus of coverage shifts toward the election as opposed to the campaign because that moves some of the control out of their hands, as the North Carolina experiment shows. You will get complaints from campaigns that their message is not getting through, or their issues are not being discussed. If we as journalists do our jobs properly and in fact do cover the campaign at some level, that complaint will be based on a disagreement about emphasis only, not exclusion, and we need not be apologetic about putting citizens' concerns ahead of politicians' and their handlers' concerns. Many studies, including those in North Carolina and Kansas, show that citizens appreciate the shift in emphasis even if the campaigns do not.

The precise effect of campaign coverage reform is difficult to measure, but efforts to quantify it are ongoing, primarily by academics. Studies in Kansas, North Carolina, Virginia and even in New Zealand offer tantalizing hints that it makes a difference in voter attitudes and, on occasion, in voter turnout. However, the efficacy of reform remains to be demonstrated as more and more news media outlets think about their role in the democratic equation.

Suggestions for Additional Reading

Michael Schudson, *"The good citizen: A history of American civic life."* New York: Free Press, 1998.
Irving Crespi, *"The public opinion process: How the people speak."* Mahwah, NJ: Lawrence Erlbaum Associates, 1997.

CHAPTER
14

Polling— Use and Abuse

By the middle of the last century, driven by a thirst for information and supported by the development of steadily more sophisticated computers and the universality of telephone service, researchers could measure public opinion quickly and relatively cheaply. Probability sampling was the key tool that, properly combined with computers and random-digit telephone dialing, allowed researchers to say with considerable confidence that a specific percentage of all Americans held certain beliefs or acted a certain way based on responses from only a tiny fraction of them. For instance, a properly drawn sample of 1,500 people would reflect, within a margin of error of 2.5 percent, the opinion of all 280 million Americans 95 percent of the time. In other words, it became possible to say something like this: "We know with 95 percent probability that 76 percent of Americans, if each was asked, would say they believe in ghosts."

Survey information is immensely useful in many fields. Government officials can factor public opinion data into policy decisions. Candidates seeking office can address certain issues in certain ways likely to help their candidacies and discover where their limited campaign time will yield the most votes. Advertising agencies can sniff out public sentiment and measure the effectiveness of advertising campaigns. Manufacturers can test the acceptance of their products and learn how to change them to meet public desires and needs. Institutions can use the information to plan and execute their missions. The possible applications of such aggregated information are endless, as are the possibilities of misuse and abuse.

For public affairs reporters and editors, the existence of such a tool presents important issues, both practical and ethical. As was seen in earlier chapters on positioning, effective listening for public voices is a critical part of reporting. One might be tempted to jump to the conclusion that surveys based on probability sampling would be the most efficient, broadest way of listening; they can claim, after all, to be "scientific" in a way that other modes of listening cannot. But automatic acceptance of polling data can also be a trap; polling's patina of ultimate reliability can deflect us as journalists from other important ways of public listening and rob our reporting of one level of authenticity even while providing another level.

Every method of listening, just like every method of news reporting, has its limitations. Surveys represent a large-scale, systematic way of listening to the community, but often at the expense of the depth and nuance afforded by other ways of listening to the community, such as participant observation and systematic eavesdropping in public places.

Particularly in public affairs reporting, journalists are tempted to reduce complex issues and ideas to convenient and glib sound bites and headlines when they have in hand a big glob of numbers that purports to be a "scientific survey." In this day of Internet communication, the temptations are multiplied, for a news organization with a Web site can conduct almost continuous "research" on any subject.

So it is important for public affairs journalists to have a full understanding of the potential of statistical research: both its potential to create better understanding and its potential to create absolute nonsense and misunderstanding.

SOME BASICS

Although polls and surveys are basically the same kind of instruments, professionals make a distinction between the two. A poll usually consists of relatively few questions and is administered over a short time span, two or three days or less, to a sample of a few hundred people. It is usually designed to get a few pieces of information quickly, such as a news media poll that seeks to gauge a political race or test public sentiment on an issue. The residual information that can reliably be teased out of polling data is limited because of the device's built-in limitations. A survey usually is more extensive and is the sort of work done by academics, established professional organizations and governments. Sample sizes can run into the tens of thousands (for instance, the Bureau of Labor Statistics' unemployment survey contacts 60,000 households each month), can involve questionnaires that take an hour or more to complete, and the interviewing schedule is much longer, weeks or even months.

Surveys can be of several kinds. The most universally accepted distinctions among surveys designs are these:

- Cross-sectional: This design shares a characteristic of most polls—a single sample of people is asked a set of questions one time. Because so many polls are conducted these days, especially national samples of voters, any enterprising reporter could piece together a portrait of sentiment over time (a longitudinal study). But this must be done with great care. The essential caveat is that the set of polls assembled for this portrait-over-time of a population must be identical. That is, they must not only be samples of the same population, but they also must have asked identical questions and employed identical interviewing and analysis techniques. Otherwise, one is wandering into an "apples and oranges" situation despite the superficial appearance of similarity.
- Longitudinal: The same questions are asked of several independent samples several times. This can provide insight into changing attitudes over time and different populations.
- Panel: The same sample of people are interviewed at different points in time, with some or all of the questions repeated. This can provide a look at changing attitudes over time in the same group and allows exploration of the reasons why individual attitudes or opinions change or do not change.

All reliable surveys and polls share one important characteristic: they begin with a probability sample. In a probability sample, each element in the universe being sampled has a known chance of being included. In most public opinion polls, known chance actually means equal chance. That is, every adult member of the population has an equal chance of being selected for an interview. If the population of interest is voters in Dallas, Texas and one wishes to obtain a representative picture of their opinions, then every registered voter should have an equal chance of being included in the survey. If the population of interest is presidents of American universities, one might want to weight the selection process according to the enrollment of each university so that the president of the University of Texas at Austin, which has 50,000 students, would have a greater chance of selection than the president of a university with 3,600 students. Whether to weight or not would depend on the goals of the survey. In either event, weighted or equal chances of selection, the probability of selection would be known for each member of the population.

To repeat, for most public opinion polls and surveys, each member of the public should have an equal chance of being selected. For this situation, Phillip Meyer and David J. Olson described the process for achieving equality this way:

> Imagine a barrel containing 25,000 black marbles and 25,000 white marbles. If the marbles were thoroughly stirred so that you could draw from the barrel blindfolded

with each marble having an equal chance of being drawn, you would not have to pull out very many before realizing that the distribution of black marbles and white marbles was about equal. From the well-established laws of probability theory, we can calculate that a sample of 370 marbles drawn in such a manner would reflect the true 50/50 division within a 5 percent margin of error nineteen times out of twenty. A larger barrel requires only a slightly larger sample. Increasing the marble population to infinity would require increasing the sample to no more than 384 for the same level of accuracy.[1]

The reason that probability sampling is a required component of reliable survey design is because it allows the calculation of a margin of error—in the marble-barrel example within 5 percent 19 times out of 20. Without a probability sample and random selection from within that sample, there can be no confidence about the results because statistical reliability is impossible.

The margin of error in a survey is important to know for a simple reason: Using sampling technique rather than surveying everyone in a given population automatically introduces a potential for error and one needs to know the size of that potential error. For instance, think about a poll of 1,500 people across the nation that has a margin of error or plus or minus 2.5 percent. If the poll shows that 75 percent of the people support Proposition A, and 21 percent are against it, with 4 percent undecided or having no opinion, one can be safe in concluding that a substantial majority of people are in support of Proposition A. If, however, the result on a question about Proposition B is that 52 percent favor it, 44 percent are opposed, and 4 percent are undecided or have no opinion, we have a much different situation. Applying the margin of error of plus or minus 2.5 percent, the result could actually be that 48 percent favor, and 48 percent are opposed—or any combination of results within those parameters. The undecideds then become a very important unknown. With such a result, one cannot declare the status of Proposition B with any assurance at all. One can only say that it's "too close to call."

Without a known margin of error based on a probability sample, one can have zero confidence in the results, even results that appear to be clear-cut, such as 80-20. Thus, "polls" and "surveys" that merely compile and index information (the "top ten universities") or that invite participation on a self-selecting basis by the respondents (vote for the best hamburger in town) are not valid. The respondents represent only themselves—and sometimes themselves many times over because there is usually no limit on the number of times that one can express an opinion in such "polls." There is no way to gauge the fit between these results and the true pattern within the public. Editors and news directors sometimes slyly acknowledge this lack of validity with qualifying words such as *unscientific* but justify their use anyway on the basis of their "human interest" or "entertainment" value. These are poor excuses for disseminating misleading—and often fraudulent and blatantly promotional—information.

---

[1]Olson and Meyer, "*To keep the republic*," p. 149.

When such techniques are applied to important public issues, the fraud is even more egregious. CNN regularly asks public opinion on its Web site. Such self-selecting polling violates every known tenet of reliable research, yet the network regularly reports the results on its newscasts. CNN carefully notes "This is not a scientific poll," but that caveat falls far short of honest disclaimer. "Not scientific" means nothing. The CNN polls are not statistically reliable, but can you imagine a network reporting on a poll and then saying, 'Oh, by the way, this information is not reliable?"

APPLYING THE BASICS

Reporters and editors interested in using polling data either as news stories or as background for news stories or decision making need to understand that reliable survey work is based on a complex set of ideas and assumptions that must mesh perfectly. In a poll's conception (What does the poll attempt to find out, and who wants to find it out?), design (How will it be discovered?), execution (Are established protocols closely followed?), interpretation (What does the data mean?), and purpose (Why are we doing this?) lie many potential hazards. A weakness in any part of the process can poison the outcome and render the data at best irrelevant and at worst misleading. A bias or predisposition can be accidentally (or intentionally, in cases of outright dishonesty) introduced at any point.

A nationally known researcher, discussing the real possibility of dishonest opinion research, said wryly, "Tell me the numbers you want and I can design a survey to get them." He was obviously aware, for example, of the differences that can be obtained in the results by how the question is worded. Think of all those biased questionnaires you have as Americans received over the years that clearly indicated what answer the sponsor wanted most people to give.

Therefore, reporters and editors dealing with polling data must answer in the positive one of two basic questions: Do we know the people and institution involved in the poll and trust their lack of bias? Or, failing that, do we know enough about the poll itself to trust the outcome? Even having a positive answer to one of those two questions about the production of the data, however, does not reach the matter of interpretation: What does the data really mean? What are we to make of the outcome?

When considering whether to use polling data, the following are some questions to ask at each step along the way.

Conception

Who wants to know, and why? Self-serving polls are much more common these days than objective ones. This does not mean that a poll by a self-serving business or institution is bound to be untrustworthy on its face, for businesses and institutions need reliable data. But knowing the "who" and "why" and "what" are important in deciding how much, if any, credence to put in the results.

Is the survey asking people about what they believe, or about what they have done or will do? The difference is important. Although beliefs do change over time, people tend to be honest about them; they will tell surveyors what they think even if the response only represents their view of the moment. Somewhat less reliance can be placed on what people say they have done and will do. For instance, if polls show that teen-age drug use is declining, does that reflect actual behavior, or does it reflect a changing attitude about what's "hip" to say? It is important to remember that polls reflect only what people say about either their beliefs or their actions, not what actually happened or will happen. A classic example is following an election in which the recorded turnout was, say, 45 percent; you will almost always find that a much higher percentage of people answer that they voted.

Design

In the case of polls attempting to measure opinion in a specific population (the nation, a state, a city), does every person in that population have a known chance of being included? Is the sampling truly random rather than self-selected? In the case of polls of smaller populations, is the group properly defined, and again, does everyone in the group have a known chance of being included?

Wording of Questions

The wording of the questions is, of course, crucial. Does the wording include potential bias? In recent political campaigns something called "push polling" has become popular with some political operatives. Push polling involves wording questions in a way that invites a particular outcome or conveys a negative message: "Would you favor a candidate who wants to do away with Social Security?" might be a legitimate question, or it might be a way of suggesting that the opposing candidate would do so, whether or not that's the case. Push polling is the most egregious, but not the only, way that bias can be introduced in the wording of the questions.

Does the wording force the respondent into too-limited a choice and thus invite error? In the 1999 to 2000 presidential campaign, Harvard University's Joan Shorenstein Center discovered a major discrepancy in traditional political polling. For decades, pollsters have read the list of candidates and asked whom the respondent favored. Usually, a small percentage of people—numbering in single digits—say they are undecided. This method, heavily relied on by the news media, conjures up a picture of a nation of potential voters who, months ahead of the election, have made up their minds. News stories appear saying that Sen. Smith is ahead of Gov. Jones, 58 percent to 36 percent, with 6 percent undecided. Such claimed results affect both the campaigns and, it is argued, some voters: a "bandwagon effect" and an "underdog effect" have both been demonstrated. The negative effects of such pronouncements are large and we deal with them later in more detail.

The Shorenstein Center discovered an important phenomenon simply by asking the question a different way in its weekly national polls.[2] "Which candidate do you support at this time, or haven't you picked a candidate yet?" was the standard question. Asking that way produced a much different picture, an electorate that was in the process of making up its mind. Over the period of November 1999 through February 2000, for example, the percentage of undecided in the Shorenstein poll ranged from a high of 74 to a one-week low of 58. The undecided number moved up and down according to how much the presidential race had been at the top of the news, but with that one-week exception at 58 percent, hovered at two-thirds or more. Of those who had made up their minds, Gov. George W. Bush was the favorite, but his figures ran consistently less than 20 percent, while the other contenders' figures were in single digits. By contrast, traditional polls by political and news organizations that virtually forced a choice showed, over the same period, Bush with more than 50 percent and his main opponent, John McCain, in the high thirties, with relatively few respondents undecided.

Although intuitively the Shorenstein design seems more likely to reflect reality months before an election, one need not decide here which method is the most reliable in order to understand clearly that the way a question is asked has huge impact on the outcome.

Execution

Were all protocols followed? What was the response rate among those selected? This has become a crucial issue with the proliferation of polling, particularly by telephone. In recent years, businesses have turned heavily to telemarketing—randomly calling people to try to sell products and services. Sometimes these telemarketers disguise their sales pitches as surveys ("We're doing a survey to find out how many people have put aluminum siding on their homes."). The deluge of commercial activity, often focused around the dinner hours when people are more likely to be at home, has con-

---

[2]Vanishing Voter Project, Joan Shorenstein Center on the Press, Politics and Public Policy at Harvard University, *http://www.vanishingvoter.org* (Retrieved October 19, 2000).

tributed, along with other factors, to a sharp rise in refusals, what researchers call the nonresponse rate. What this means is that when response rates
are low—especially when they are less than 50 percent—those who do respond are, in effect, a self-selected sample that may not represent the population at large.

How were refusals handled? How many times were they called back in an
effort to maintain the integrity of the sample? Think about what kinds of
persons are most likely to consent to an interview on the first phone call to
their homes and what kinds of persons are least likely to be reached on that
first phone call. Are they likely to be people with similar schedules, temper-
aments and occupations, or are they likely to be quite different? Most reliable survey organizations try to reach specific people or households three to
five times before changing the sample by substituting another name or number. Such rigor adds greatly to the cost.

Interpretation

This is where art (and journalism) impose themselves on the rigors of research science, even if the research is done perfectly. How the data is presented—its context and how the story is framed—can overinterpret or
underexplain and therefore distort even the most reliable data.

Bear in mind that most polls are simply a snapshot of a moment in time. It
may say nothing at all about what went on before that moment or what may
go on later. The responses are more often reflexive than deliberative, and
therefore may reflect a transient environmental factor. For instance, a poll
on gun control done in the wake of the Washington, D.C. area sniper killings
may reflect the emotional response of the moment more than it reflects beliefs, particularly among the majority of people who feel some ambivalence
about the issue.

Timing is crucial, both as to the environment in which the poll is taken
and in its proximity to an event. Perhaps the most famous political polling
snafu of all time—the unanimous declaration by pollsters that Thomas
Dewey would defeat Harry Truman for president in 1948—was in part at-
tributable to the fact that polling stopped in mid-October and thus did not
catch a last-week shift away from Dewey to Truman. This, in turn, set up the
photo of the broadly grinning president-elect Truman on the day after the
election holding up a *Chicago Daily Tribune* with the unfortunate, poll-
based headline "Dewey Defeats Truman." Even Truman had gone to bed on
election night convinced that he had lost, so persuasive was the effect of the
polling. Researchers, politicians and journalists all learned important lessons from that calamity.

What does the poll really say? Again, the questionable but popular practice of political horse-race polling as a way of creating news provides a negative example. Most such polls ask, "If the election were held today, would

you vote for Candidate Smith or Candidate Jones?" Wording the question that way avoids the problem of asking people to predict what they will do in the future and thus pollsters defend it as legitimate. But such polls are often reported by journalists as projecting the leading candidate to win or that the leading candidate is ahead, as in a horse race. As with an actual horse race, nothing matters until the finish line: election day. A snapshot of the position of the horses in the backstretch will get you nothing at the betting window. Much can, and probably will, change before the finish. This raises an interesting question: What lasting value, except for political strategists, lies in knowing on Sept. 6 who would have won an election on Sept. 5 when the real election is Nov. 5? Is the poll answering a question that no one has asked?

It is ironic that journalists make the heaviest use of polling at its most vulnerable time and condition—calling the horse race as the candidates head toward election day. Not only are many citizens truly undecided right up until election day, but many (unfortunately, even in national elections only about half) will wind up not voting at all. Any poll that purports to call the horse race and estimate its outcome must also have figured out who will actually vote and who will not. This is not an easy task. Simply asking people if they intend to vote or if they have voted in the past can result in distortions. Sorting out likely voters from unlikely voters in the sample interviewed remains more art than science.

Another trap that journalists, particularly time-pinched television journalists, fall into when reporting poll results is oversimplification. Most television newscasts now at least refer to the margin of error and the sample size when reporting that Gov. Smith is leading Sen. Jones 52 percent to 38 percent with 10 percent undecided. The graphics normally show those figures prominently, however, and any reference to the margin of error—which could put another, just as likely outcome at a much closer 48 percent to 42 percent—is in small type, and the newscasters rarely "do the math" for viewers to explain fully the other possible outcomes. Thus, the casual viewer is left with an erroneous impression of precision (and candidate momentum) that simply doesn't reside in the poll data.

Related to this trap is one of failure to deal with what researchers call "the marginals," the further breakdown of the respondent sample into subgroups, which can actually change the interpretation of the results. Michael Traugott and Paul Lavrakas, in their useful book "*The Voter's Guide to Election Polls*," illustrated the perils of failing to deal with marginals with this cautionary tale:

Questions were raised early in the 1992 primaries about Bill Clinton's fidelity after a woman held a press conference and claimed she had had an affair with him. In response to the press conference, many news organizations sponsored or conducted polls asking questions about the public's view of a candidate who had been unfaithful to his wife. Most of those polls showed that a majority of Americans felt that such a person would not make a good candidate, and many journalists subsequently concluded that the Clinton candidacy was in trouble.

Subsequent analysis (of the marginals) suggested that those who were most concerned about the fidelity issue were Republicans and others who had already decided to support George Bush. People who had decided to support Clinton were less concerned. It also turned out that people who were registered to vote were less concerned than unregistered citizens. When analyzed in this fashion, the poll suggested that the Clinton candidacy was probably not in trouble, especially since the allegations had not been proven at that time.[3]

Accurate interpretation necessarily involves much more than looking at the primary numbers that a poll produces. Deepening the analysis also, of course, can make for a less dramatic-sounding story. As the old newspaper ironic saying goes, "You check around too much, you screw up a good story."

As will be seen, however, failing to check around enough—to not look for the true meaning of poll results and search for alternative interpretations—raises serious ethical issues that go to the very heart of the role of journalism in democracy.

Finally, we as journalists must ask, as we should in all of our journalistic efforts, "What's the purpose, what are we trying to accomplish?" It is not an irrelevant question, though it is one that makes some journalists uncomfortable ("We're not trying to accomplish anything except telling news," many insist.) But the agenda-setting role of the news media, deliberate or inadvertent, is well known and understood as we saw in Chapter 5 (this volume) so the question must be faced squarely and honestly.

After all, isn't journalism something more than telling good stories that happen to have some factual basis? The topics that journalists select influence the focus of public attention, and the way that journalists present those topics influences how the public thinks and talks about the topics. These are powerful agenda-setting roles that cannot be avoided. Whatever is selected for the daily news influences the public agenda, sometimes, directly by influencing the importance of these items among the people, sometimes in the case of topics that the public regards as trivial or irrelevant, by deflecting attention from more significant aspects of public life.

NECESSARY PRECAUTIONS

A fundamental problem is that rigorously done survey research and high-pressure daily journalism are not a good marriage. Journalism has relatively little interest in what was true eight weeks ago or eight months ago. Rigorously done survey research and sound interpretation of it requires

---

[3]Michael Traugott and Paul Lavrakas, *"The voter's guide to election polls."* New York: Chatham House, 2000, p. 116.

time. Yet a courtship and a marriage, of sorts, between journalism and survey research was consummated in the last decades of the 20th century.

In the '40s and '50s, the research on political campaigns was done by independent, specialized institutions. With only an occasional revealed failure (the Truman–Dewey presidential campaign being the most notorious), institutions such as Gallup and Roper and Yankelovich prospered. Many newspapers and broadcast outlets subscribed to those surveys and turned them into news stories, but the services were expensive and the news organizations all had the same, prepackaged results.

With the development of telephone surveying techniques and the proliferation of computer databases, news organizations and political operations realized that there could be advantages in doing their own polling. It could be done in-house at reasonable cost and could produce exclusive material on the schedule and with the content that the institutions preferred.

Clearly, for news organizations, such information made for interesting reading. Knowing who was ahead months before the election presented a tantalizing array of possibilities beyond the mere recitation of the statistics of the moment. It opened to political reporters a new and simple way, for instance, to analyze campaign tactics by juxtaposing them against the backdrop of the "hard numbers." This, in turn, invited the cynical assumption that whatever a candidate did or said was grounded at least as much in those hard numbers as in principle. It also attributed movement and drama to what otherwise might be a dry electoral landscape of issues and expressed intentions that only a truly conscientious voter or a political junkie could love.

Political organizations also jumped on board the bandwagon. If they could know the status of the race, perhaps they could react in ways that could move the numbers in the direction they preferred, find gaps in their opponents' armor, and develop strategies to meet public desires and requirements.

Political and news institutions began zipping along the edge of a very steep and crumbly ethical cliff, for, as we have shown, reliable survey work is expensive, time-consuming, complex, and wholly reliant on independence and honesty. (Recall the wry quote, "Tell me what numbers you want and I can do a survey to produce them.") Textbooks used in journalism research courses, conferences, and the publication of standards have tried to ensure that the public is informed of the limitations of survey research. The American Association for Public Opinion Research may be given much of the credit for the limited mention of sample size and statistical margin of error in some news reports, but for the most part, the limitations are ignored in favor of broad, unsupportable declarations.

With what can only be considered willful ignorance given what is widely known today about the limits of surveying, the news media and political operatives, sometimes separately, sometimes in association, are frighteningly undeterred by such details of candor and research rigor. They plunge ahead

with quickie, underfunded surveys that purport to measure all sorts of senti-
ments that are instantly reported as revealed truth, losing sight of the fact
that the old saying about computers—garbage in garbage out—applies
equally to public opinion research.

So ardent and reckless has been journalism's love affair with statistical research that broadcast stations and local magazines regularly set out in search of
"the city's best hamburger" or "the city's best dry cleaner," asking viewers and
readers to "cast their vote" on an 800 number or online or by clipping and send-
ing in a coupon. What happens, of course, is ballot stuffing by employees, owners and promoters. These clearly promotional "surveys" are sometimes, but not
always, labeled nonscientific but nevertheless are reported as meaningful.

The rush to measure sophisticated concepts with cheap, rough tools and
report them as absolutes creates problems of polarization, pollution and diversion that further damage the news media's credibility and undermine its
role in the democratic process. Among the effects are the following:

- It polarizes opinion on issues and thereby restricts useful discussion of
  them. If 51 percent of people are reported to be in favor of Proposition
  A, 39 percent are said to be opposed, and 10 percent are undecided, the
  issue is rendered as poured concrete. People who harbor some measure
  of ambivalence—and that's most people on most issues —are reduced
  to reveling in their place in the majority or sulking in their role in the minority. Persuasion and conversion become much more difficult; deliberation and exchange are discouraged because the issue seems settled.
- It pollutes sound policy-making by weakening the concept of representative government, which is supposed to balance faithful representation of
  constituent wishes against detailed information not always known to con-
  stituents, personal judgment and moral conviction. Increasingly, elected
  representatives seem to rely on polls to determine their votes, which has
  the effect of removing that important guard against the potential tyranny
  of the majority. Sen. Patrick Moynihan put it differently, but just as firmly,
  in an interview in *Civilization*, "We've lost (in the Congress) our sense of
  ideas that we stand by, principles that are important to us … I think you
  wouldn't be mistaken, as a citizen, to ask: Are we really necessary?"[4]
- It pollutes the surveying environment itself. At least some part of the
  falling response rates can be attributed to survey fatigue. How many "I
  just want to ask you a few questions" calls can the nation hang up on at
  the dinner hour before the results become wholly invalid?
- It pollutes the political environment. Campaign money has a notorious
  nose for the numbers, so candidates with bad numbers are starved out

---

[4]Quoted in Peter Jennings, American voices: How polls have trampled the Constitution,
Civilization, 7, No. 7 (August–September 1999), p. 68.

early in the process, as demonstrated in early fall of 1999 by the early withdrawal of several Republican presidential candidates.

• It diverts, even subverts, the process of public life by positioning citizens as spectators to a contest decided, or being decided, somewhere else rather than positioning them as potential participants in decision making.

• It diverts electoral-campaign reportage from its true mission. It's easier and feels more dynamic to write about the horse race than to deal with issues. It also tempts reporters to frame most political positions as being in response to numbers rather than in reliance on values and principles, driving people away from politics rather than engaging them in it. This is not to say that election coverage should ignore reliable polling data, which does create a level of interest in some people. Problems arise when polling data on the horse race becomes the core of coverage to the exclusion of more substantive and engaging matters.

The polarization, pollution and diversion created by overreliance on, sometimes sloppy acquiring of, and careless reporting of survey data should raise serious ethical questions for journalists and citizens. Given what is known—though not always admitted—about the limitations of most surveys done by news media organizations and political parties, it is irresponsible not to face those questions.

Ethical questions arise because the passing off of quickie surveys as revealed truth does harm, including the harms catalogued previously. Ethical questions also arise because too often the surveys create news where there is none by disguising, deliberately or through lack of understanding, statistical ambiguity as certainty.

There is no easy way out of the dilemma. Truthfully describing the methodology, including all its attendant caveats about margin of error, sampling techniques, question wording, response rate and so on, would reveal much of the information as meaningless. And, of course, it wouldn't feel like news.

News media outlets combining resources—sometimes with other institutions—to make reliable independent research affordable is an idea that some have adopted at a limited level. But even unlimited financial resources and the involvement of reliable, independent research institutions cannot address two major problems:

• The old struggle of immediacy versus accuracy. Journalists and political operatives aren't interested in who was ahead eight weeks ago; they want to know who is ahead this morning, whether that is knowable or not.

• The poor, superficial and unthinking reporting and editing of the results, which is the core problem.

None of this is intended to condemn the proper use of surveys and other statistical analysis in journalism. In fact, the tying together of large, independent databases by high-speed computers has led to the development of an important journalistic specialty, "computer-assisted journalism." Rigorous analysis of information from multiple sources had led to much important reporting in the last decade.

Nor does any of this suggest that quantitative research is fundamentally flawed or not of value and importance. As with most things in life, one gets out of it what one puts into it. Good research of any kind is expensive and time-consuming, and its results require careful interpretation.

Surveys are more properly used for ascertaining public concerns and priorities in the maelstrom of contemporary public life and as the foundation of serious investigative reporting, not as a source of spot news. Journalism is supposed to tell people what is known about things of relevance. The present state of survey coverage suggests serious rethinking of both criteria: Do we really "know" what we claim to know, and does it matter?

Suggestions for Additional Reading

Michael Traugott and Paul Lavrakas, *"The voter's guide to election polls."* New York: Chatham House, 2000.

A Map of the Future

What will the public affairs journalism of 2010 and 2020 look like? Will the trends in its style and tone that dominated the last two decades of the 20th century begin to wane and some emerging trends gain momentum in the 21st century?

It will be surprising if that is not the case because otherwise it would be contrary to more than 150 years of American journalism history. Dipping into the continuous stream of journalistic evolution at 30-year intervals has consistently revealed evolutionary changes that, week to week and even year to year, are invisible. Indeed, 30 years—the approximate time it takes for a generation to move from puberty to mature adulthood, to move from learners to leaders—has been for centuries about the amount of time it takes for new ideas to gain firm footing in any culture.

Changes in journalism, as was seen in Chapter 4's (this volume) discussion of this historical evolution, have been driven by the confluence of three major factors: new developments in technology, changing social conditions, and creative and entrepreneurial impulses.

Late in the 20th century, different ideas about public affairs journalism began to be expressed and implemented by some newspaper and broadcast journalists and discussed and researched by academics. Those ideas form the foundations of this book. Whether those ideas will come to define public affairs journalism remains for others to discover when they take one of those 30-year dips into the evolutionary stream one or two decades from now. It is clear, however, that the ideas that began to be expressed in the early 1990s are both in harmony with and in part driven by developments in technology, changes in social conditions and creative impulses over the past few decades.

TECHNOLOGICAL DEVELOPMENTS

The conundrum of the technology-driven information explosion is that everyone now has the potential to know almost everything and, as a consequence, everyone is in danger of knowing nothing that is of social or public value. Consider Harold, the Rutabaga Man. Harold is only interested in rutabagas, but he is avidly interested in everything about them: the genetics, the history, growing them, cooking them, and their role in various cultures. His PC allows him access to all the world's knowledge of rutabagas, but most important, it allows him to filter out all other information on any topic whatsoever because he is in total control of the keyboard. No information can impinge on his life that he does not will; and he does not will anything other than rutabaga information.

Blessedly, there are few Harolds. But the reality of greater and greater information specialization—the potential narrowness of possessed knowledge amid the vastness of the information universe—renders vulnerable the concept of shared, relevant information that is crucial to democratic deliberation.

How can public affairs journalists of the future cope with the conundrum? One way is by learning to deal across the lines of media, to exploit the potential of the convergence theory of news presentation. Increasingly, journalism schools and news organizations are finding ways to erase the artificial lines between print and broadcast and Internet. Convergence offers economic as well as presentational incentives, for fewer hands can do more simply by knowing how to manipulate the same information for various formats.

A major byproduct of this convergence will be an even more powerful and more homogenous news agenda, a situation that makes it imperative that the media agenda provide useful information rather than transitory diversion for the public. For most of their history, the mass media have been more adept at providing us with knowledge of public affairs rather than knowledge about public affairs.[1] Even today the news media are far more adept at signaling significant changes in the environment than in educating the public about significant changes in the environment. However, the convergence of the traditional mass media in tandem with a rich array of Web sites makes it feasible to serve both functions. Success in achieving either goal, knowledge of or knowledge about public affairs, is dependent, of course, on understanding what will resonate with contemporary audiences as significant public affairs news.

CHANGING SOCIAL CONDITIONS

Whether one agrees with Robert Putnam that America's civic culture deteriorated in the last half of the 20th century, or with Michael Schudson that it

---

[1]Robert Park, News as a form of knowledge, *American Journal of Sociology*, 45 (1940), 667–686.

simply changed, the potential audience that journalism attempted to address in that period was clearly not the one it had addressed in previous decades. And for most of the last half of the century, journalism failed to recognize and react to the difference.

Only when newspaper readership and news broadcast viewership began to decline precipitously in the last two decades of the century did journalists —in contrast to their already concerned owners and bosses—start to pay attention and ask why. As those trends first began to become clear in the 1980s, the response of many news media outlets was to try to chase readers and viewers into the narrow and specialized niches into which they were retreating. That effort failed to stem the leakage because most newspapers and broadcast outlets did not have the resources to provide meaningful content addressing the vast and growing array of special and narrowing interests exhibited by the departing readers and viewers. Newspapers and broadcast newsrooms were simply not equipped to be all things to all people in any meaningful way. The effort to chase down those departing consumers led to a pattern of trivialization in news content and the blurring of lines between news and entertainment.

When it became clear that those marketing efforts were not working, advertisers began to seek alternative ways to reach the former readers and viewers, and the resource issue for newsrooms was exacerbated. Making the situation even more dire was the acceleration through the 1970s and 1980s of group ownership by publicly held companies. Wall Street, with its imperative for annual earnings growth, demonstrated little patience with companies that could not produce higher and higher returns. Corporate leaders began to squeeze newsroom staffs and resources such as newsprint as journalism began to be regarded in corporate offices and on Wall Street as an expense to be minimized rather than a resource that could help grow the overall business of a newspaper or broadcast outlet.

Researchers and analysts continue to argue over why Americans were retreating into their private lives, and hundreds of analyses have been offered. But it was clear that the American public was retreating and that many aspects of public life, including the idea of mass media, were being negatively affected. Voter participation declined. The gap between rich and poor widened, leading to a rise in the politics of resentment. The information explosion resulted not in broader knowledge but narrower knowledge. Participation in traditional, broad-based civic organizations plummeted, although citizen involvement in short-lived, action-oriented, narrow-purposed and ever-changing affinity groups grew. To that extent, Putnam's decline and Schudson's change were not mutually exclusive concepts.

As people turned more toward their own goods and were less openly concerned about the broader public good, their appetite for and use of news changed. Schudson labeled them monitorial citizens, people who scanned rather than read newspapers and who filtered newscasts. Information that was not clearly a personal threat or opportunity was instantly set aside. This public was observing the environment more than they were in the environment. The extent of the damage that change would do to civic life is also subject to debate. But one thing was clear: Institutions of all sorts were increasingly out of favor. Survey ratings for government, the news media, television, politicians and political parties, and many professions were less than favorable. In 1994, 71 percent of Americans agreed with the statement, "The news media stand in the way of society solving its problems."

Clearly, as the 20th century ended, public life and journalism were facing huge challenges. During much of that century, the audiences of the news media—which is to say, the vast majority of Americans—also had been significantly involved in key aspects of public life. But in the final decades of the century this ebbing symbiosis demanded a significant rethinking of how the news media are edited and produced and of how a new generation of journalists is educated on the campus.

ENTREPRENEURIAL AND CREATIVE IMPULSES

The ideas that comprise the body of this book arose largely in response to the technological and social changes just discussed. Journalists concerned about the status of democracy and their craft as the 20th century drew to a close began to talk and think about ways to address the dual problem of citizen disengagement from public life and public dissatisfaction with the performance of the news media.

The impetus was in part entrepreneurial, that is, driven by the need to address the severe decline in newspaper readership and broadcast news viewership. If there was a way to halt the downward spiral, it clearly had something to do with the fact that the content of newscasts and newspapers simply wasn't compelling enough. That's where entrepreneurial impulses and creative impulses began to merge.

What if, some journalists began to think, we could create a form of journalism that attacked the interconnected problems of citizen disengagement from public life and dissatisfaction with the news media's performance? A journalism that was not market driven in the sense of chasing readers and viewers, but rather was engagement driven? Might not that serve several good purposes, including even easing the problem of declining profits that was threatening the entire profession?

In the 1990s, having made some fundamental mental shifts, many journalists began to experiment along those lines. One mental shift was to recognize that, whether we like the idea or not or are comfortable with it, journalism is unavoidably a participant, a "player" if you will, in public affairs. The agenda-setting role of the news media is undeniable. The only question is which values journalists will bring to their role as participants.

That shift leads unavoidably to a second one: that our agenda-setting role imposes an obligation on us to do journalism in ways that are calculated to help public life go well by re-engaging people in it. Public life going well means that democracy succeeds in answering the question, "What shall we do?" The answer, in a democracy, should be determined by informed and engaged citizens.

Expressing those mental shifts in our journalism requires bringing to bear a set of values in addition to the traditional values of professional objectivity, fairness, balance, accuracy, responsibility and truth telling. Those additional values are:

- Moving away from detachment; that is, remembering that we are citizens as well as journalists, stakeholders in a process that needs our presence as useful participants.
- Seeing our job as not only describing what is going wrong, but also imagining what going right might be like and offering citizens that vision. That is, focusing on the possibilities of solutions to problems rather than simply the problems.
- That, in turn, requires that we see conflict in its actual multidimensional terms rather than its contrived bipolar terms and see it as a means toward resolution rather than an end in itself.
- Moving away from the idea of readers and viewers as consumers or spectators or victims to the idea of regarding them as a public, as potential actors in arriving at democratic solutions to public problems, moving toward the idea of helping to build the public's capacity to talk about and form solutions.

The intellectual and ethical principle in which all these ideas and the future of journalism reside is that the medium in which journalism is done—on paper, on the airwaves, on the Internet, through broadband, or in some ways as yet unimagined—is far less important than the manner in which it is performed (the What). And the manner it is performed is less important than the reason we do it (the Why).

Author Index

Subject Index

A

Agenda setting, 41–49, 88, 92, 150
    and ethics, 54–59
    possible decline, 65

C

Charlotte, NC, 115–116
Charlotte Observer, 115, 125
Civic mapping, 103–104
Clinton, B., 94

D

Deliberation, 94, 106–118, 126–127
    see also Public judgment
    and power, 113–114
    characteristics, 110
    Charlotte, NC, 115–116
    compared with discussion, debate and
        dialogue, 106–109
    layers of civic life, 101–102
    Texas, 116–117

E

Elections, 119–130

F

First amendment, 9–18

H

Hamilton, A., 13
Harwood Group, 101, 103
Hutchins Commission, 57–58

I

Information explosion, xii–xiii, 80–81

J

Joan Shorenstein Center at Harvard University, 137–138
Journalism, *see also* News values and
    norms, Public listening
    and democracy, xii, xiv–xv, 8, 9–18,
        29–30, 86–88, 91–105,
        120–121, 150
    detached observation, 91–92, 104
    disconnect with citizens, 100–101,
        122–123, 129–130
    dual facets, ix
    gatekeeping values, 92
    historical evolution, 31–39, 146–150
    master narratives, 124
    reforming election coverage, 123–129
    rules for achieving public judgment,
        96–100
    watchdog role, 52–54

K

Kettering Foundation, 103, 109, 113

155